A LEGACY COLLECTION:

Bits and Pieces from a Life

KEN FELLOWS

A Legacy Collection: Bits and Pieces from a Life

Copyright © 2017 by Ken Fellows

All rights reserved. No part of this book may be reproduced without the express permission of the author, except in the case of brief excerpts embodied in critical articles and reviews.

Published by Piscataqua Press

An imprint of RiverRun Bookstore, Inc.

142 Fleet Street

Portsmouth, NH 03801

www.riverrunbookstore.com

www.piscataquapress.com

ISBN: 978-1-944393-75-5

Printed in the United States of America

It steadies me to tell these things.

Seamus Heaney

This mosaic of life experiences, reminiscences, and musings is dedicated to dearest Kristin, our beloved Ian, Maria, Hannah, Jesse and Ella, and to so many close friends. Thank you for being my steadfast support and constant inspiration.

TABLE OF CONTENTS

INTRODUCTION	
My Legacy Writing	1
Legacy Writing's Not Easy	3
FAMILY	
"How I Met Your Mother"	9
Wedding Day	13
River Trip	16
Dad	20
Brother Rick	24
Missing	28
Snapshot	32
Ian Edward Fellows Recollections	36
Being a Grandfather	45
Strawberries and Grandparents	48
I'm a Grandpa	51
One Best Friend	54
Dear Mary Lou	57
Ella Works the Playground	60
Ella Goodnight	62
An International Adoption	65
Prodigal Child	69
MEMORIES	
Growing Up I	75
Growing Up II	79
Growing Up III	82
Movies at Home	86
My Life in Music	89
Auditorium Dread	92
Christmas Present	96

Tight Spots	98
Grill Guy	102
Memorable Mentor	106
Camp Doc	109
The Joy of Raspberries	113
20th and Spruce	116
Deux Chem Trilogy I	120
Deux Chem Trilogy II	124
Deux Chem Trilogy III	129
Don't Hold Dinner	133
Lagnes Days	137
Walk in the Rachel Carson Woods	140
Symphony Hall Echo	142
One Old Truck	145
Roger and I	149
Kerala	152
Stairwell Lessons	156
Thanks, Dewitt	159
At Sea	163
Sister "C"	169

REFLECTIONS

Coming of Age	175
Catcher in the Rye and Me	179
Public Humor	185
A Diagonal Moment	187
Uncomfortable with Uncertainty	190
Perusing the Newspaper	193
Compulsive	196
Daydreaming	199
Quiet Car	203
Journey	206
Saying Goodbye	209
Diminished Faculty	214
Obituary	217

Changing	223
Obstetrics Intern	227
50 Years Together	232

Thoughts, Clippings, and Scraps

Compromise	237
Fading Memories	241
Post Trump Election: A Letter to my Children	244

MY LEGACY WRITING

WHY THIS COLLECTION OF STORIES, ANECDOTES AND VIGNETTES? One reason: like other old people, I like recalling my life's experiences. I also enjoy reliving recollections by writing them down and talking about them. Looking back lets me feel like the elderly man who was "so old he could be any age he wanted to be."

Another excuse: the philosopher and psychologist Erik Erikson states that the fundamental task of "maturity" is to reflect on one's life. Successfully accomplished, one comes to a "philosophical acceptance; it's not just daydreaming, it's critical stuff." Without it, he surmises, there's the risk of "unmitigated regret and bitterness." Fortunately, I reflect on my life with general equanimity and some smiles.

I've been careful in my approach. Mark Twain noted; "When I was young I could remember anything, whether it happened or not; but I am old and soon I shall remember only the latter."

Even though I've been as factual as possible, I have not attempted to create a life's "Memoir' here, a project that would entail an organized presentation of my life in more detail and with clearer personal lessons. My intent has been less ambitious. I've written a series of descriptive recollections of parts of my life, primarily for their entertainment value. I hope also that my children and grandchildren will glean some idea of what my youth was like, what I did as an adult, how I felt about some things and what problems I confronted. I've included verbal portraits of my grandparents, parents, wife, children and friends to help promote a sense of familial and cultural continuity — my 'legacy.' That's why I like the term "Legacy Writing."

My method was simple. Stimulated by years of memoir writing classes, I chose a number of my life's experiences I wanted to describe for their humor, drama or purely 'scenic' value. I did look for a "so what" in each — a sentinel observation, a helpful guideline, a personal meaning — which I sometimes found, sometimes not. I assiduously avoided the opposite approach — choosing a life lesson or meaningful milestone, and then dredging up illustrative yarns and anecdotes. I spent much of my life teaching, but had no similar intent here. If these papers bring anyone some fun or pleasure, well, that's good.

"The universe is made up of stories... not atoms."

(Poet Muriel Rukheyser)

LEGACY WRITING'S NOT EASY

COMPOSING PIECES FOR A "LIFE'S MOSAIC" for me is fulfilling and compelling, which is why I've been devoted to it for over 10 years. But, having written nearly 80 legacy stories by now, I have some reservations.

At the top of the list: **where to stop**? Where to draw the line between what my present and future relatives might be interested in, entertained by or benefit from, and what my ego (my 'apparent self') desires in assuaging my compulsion to write. I encounter the same problem in painting—when to stop—how to know when going further will not improve the work and may even degrade it. This conflict, common to all art forms, has no resolving rules or guidelines. It seems to depend entirely on 'judgment', precarious as that may be.*

Another problem: **who's in and who's out**? When I began, I aimed to document only the experiences, events, and revelations in my life that were either unusual, amusing, or substantive life lessons. As the writing has played out, my immediate family members and a few close friends have been included, but my siblings and many friends are not represented. It's not because I don't love those left out, or don't value their part in my life. I'm not so forgetful, ungrateful or insensitive. To prevent the legacy collection from becoming too long and tiresome, some things and some dear people I have excluded. It's a necessary, but regrettable, personal compromise.

'Truth' in memoir writing is an everlasting concern and item for discussion. Pat Conroy, an acknowledged American novelist and memoirist** asserts that "fiction contains memoir, and memoir contains fiction." I prefer the distinction made by other writers between 'truth' and 'honesty' in legacy writing: *'truth' is what really happened*, the facts of the matter, whereas *'honesty' is what the author remembers having occurred*, a distinction which acknowledges the limitations of human memory. I have assiduously avoided inserting fiction in my writing, while taking refuge in admitting that my legacy pieces are certainly more 'honest' than 'truthful.'

Conroy also contemplates the connection between 'truth' and 'loss' in his writing. His book, *The Great Santini*, (a memoir about his abusive, Marine Corp father), left his sister no longer speaking to him. His defense is, "if in writing a portrait of my family...I don't talk about the effect on Carol...about how her childhood ruined her life, I'd be a liar and an unfit witness for the family. I want the truth as I know it, as I lived it. I can't tell you how much I regret losing my sister. I suffer still. When you write memoir, that's the bargain you make with God and the devil."

Fortunately, in my writing experience I've never had to make such a bargain. I can't imagine a piece of writing being more important than losing a family member or close friend. But then, I don't write for a living, just for pleasure.

In some instances, I have obscured others' character defects and personal foibles with generalities and euphemisms. Since I've asked no one's permission to include them in my pieces, I feel no right to reveal deep secrets or stir up dormant emotions. Describing past events and human interactions with relevant backstories and particular circumstances, while still protecting the privacy of those involved, is a high-wire act, and this is where I've made another compromise. I'd rather preserve intimate relationships by inserting some ambiguity than risk alienating family and friends by offering my version of the 'truth.' This derives from my Buddhist reading to avoid "dualistic thinking" — that habit of thinking that what I believe is the only answer.

I started out with the intent to leave my children and grandchildren some idea of what my life was like and what were some of my formative adventures. I want my writing to be no more complicated than that.

*"To have a great adventure, and survive, requires good judgment. Good judgment comes from experience. Experience, of course, is the result of poor judgment."
G. Tabin

**Low Country Heart: Reflections on a Writing Life - 2015

FAMILY

"HOW I MET YOUR MOTHER"

"So you're headed for duty with the Marines at El Toro. You'll probably live in nearby Laguna Beach. I know a girl there you could call. Her name is Kristin Thorsdale... 'someone I met on a blind date. She's a spoiled brat...but pretty...and smart."

I barely knew the guy telling me all this.

The Vietnam War was less than a year old in 1965, but my tour there—as a Navy doctor on a ship asked to pluck downed pilots from the Gulf of Tonkin—was over. A happy, 25 year old bachelor, I was on a small Destroyer steaming back to San Diego. My next assignment was a few miles up the California coast with the Marines at the El Toro Naval Air Station near Laguna. I was sharing a cramped 2-bunk cabin with a Navy line-officer. I didn't like him very much. He was bird-faced, unkempt, overbearing and self-important. So I disregarded his description of the girl in Laguna. But I was leery about her. Who would go out with someone like him?

As recommended by my annoying acquaintance, I did find a place to live in Laguna Beach, an attractive, hillside town/artist colony, geographically like the steep-slopped villages of the Italian Riviera. Another Navy doctor and I rented the cozy, set-back guest house of a grand, Spanish style, waterfront home once owned by Hollywood's Bette Davis and James Mason. Towering over the very edge of the Pacific, giant breakers crashed against its fortress-like, concrete foundation, the waves washing back to the sea over its own private beach.

Within a week there I hesitantly phoned Kristin Thorsdale. Reservations about her choice in men and the "bratty" characterization lingered in the back of my mind. Similarly, I wondered if she might have some qualms of her own: why wouldn't she think that I could be as peculiar as her previous blind-date Naval Officer? With all those anxieties in play, it's small wonder that we agreed to a first date the next evening.

Driving to her parents Laguna neighborhood, where she was home on vacation from Mills College, her name stirred in me visions of statuesque Viking model — an adolescent daydream of Anita Eckberg. My front-door knock was answered by her mother, who I learned afterward was very unhappy at Kristin's having accepted a blind date with "a sailor nobody knew." I was dressed in civilian clothes and must have flashed my most endearing smile. Kristin told me later; "...my mother's demeanor changed instantly. When she came to announce your arrival, her anger was gone. She had suddenly become enthusiastic."

Kristin Elizabeth Thorsdale was a 22-year-old beauty... particularly appealing with long, dark hair falling on her slim shoulders under a blue Marimekko sheath. Her dark brown eyes glowed. She was shyly nervous, modestly cool and confidently intelligent —an attractive, real replacement for my premature fantasy of a Scandinavian movie-queen.

We drove in my blue Corvette to the Sandpiper, a Laguna bar and Marine officer's hangout. In a short time there I realized that both the car and the venue were all wrong: she was an art major at Mills, a folk singing/ guitar playing/hippy whose friends were active in the anti-war/anti-establishment environs of Berkeley and San Francisco. Smitten, I had only one card to play; I was a folk music-loving/autoharp strumming/Joan Baez worshipping guy. I could at least talk that talk. So I did.

From summer 1965 thru early spring 1966 we maintained a long distance romance.

We dated whenever she was in Laguna or I drove up to Mills College in Oakland. In between were a myriad of letters and phone calls as she completed her senior college year. Her family never saw me in uniform. They began to wonder if I really was in the Navy. Her teen brother and sister dismissed me as a curious Midwestern nerd. At Mills, a women's college then, I was told the student body was of one mind; first, my Corvette had to go, then my short, military haircut and probably then some other glaring faults too.

After dating 5-6 months, I was picking her up one evening at home in Laguna. Looking at her through a window while walking up to the house, a voice in my head said; "OK, she's the one. You'd enjoy coming home to her every night." I also mentioned about the same time that I really enjoyed my bachelor life, to which she answered with a wry smile; "Yes, but you're dying inside." *What?? Was she jesting? Could that be true?* I tried to dismiss the thought, but it weighed on me. I was also feeling some 'matrimonial pressure' from her mother Peggy who began saying; "What are we going to do with Kristin when you're gone back to Boston?"

In late April 1966 we went with her family to their vacation house near Palm Springs. One warm evening we went for a moonlit walk in the desert. Caught up in the romantic aura of a soft cactus breeze, I proposed. A few days later we announced our engagement to her parents while dining at an Angel's baseball game. While her father and I watched the game, her excited mother and she made frantic wedding plans. There wasn't much time: I was to be discharged from the Navy July 7th and to report ASAP to Boston to begin my Radiology Residency. In about a week my Corvette was sold and we were driving a sensible, grey Volvo sedan, a wedding present from her parents. We were married on July 2, 1966 in Laguna, honey-mooned 3 days in Carmel, then drove cross-country to Boston. Our first tiny apartment there had no ocean view, just two windows facing the yellow brick side of a synagogue next door.

Our first fall back East we went to Cambridge one Saturday to see a Harvard-Navy football game. Wondering through a Cambridge bookstore, we gasped to see the Navy officer who had been our match-maker. He didn't' see us. We turned and scurried out of the store. We should have been excited to tell him how things worked out, but he was so strange we couldn't muster the courage. He'll never know the great story he started.

WEDDING DAY

JULY 2, 1966 WAS ONE OF THOSE GLORIOUS, sunny Southern California days where clear, salty Laguna Beach air moved on gentle, warm breezes. Everywhere garden flowers bloomed, their fragrances mixing with the ubiquitous scent of eucalyptus. A great day for our wedding.

In truth I have only a blurry recollection of the late morning ceremony itself. I do recall being nervous but not reticent. I was 'ready' as I gave Kristin's trembling hand a reassuring squeeze when we met at the Laguna Congregational Church alter.

Later that afternoon at the wedding reception I was relaxed and happy. The party with around 100 guests was an outdoor affair in the Thordales' backyard, high in the Laguna hills overlooking a sparkling silver-blue Pacific Ocean. Several generations from both families were there, meeting for the first time with grace and goodwill. I was also pleased to have many friends from medical school in Ann Arbor, an internship in Portland (OR) and a just-completed 2 years as a US Naval Medical Officer. That so many of them were residing in, or passing through, S. California at the time seems extraordinary now. The presence of a few of them can be explained by Frank Lloyd Wright's theory on why so many light-weights and misfits end up in the Southwestern corner of the US; he surmised "there must have been a continental tilt, and anything that wasn't nailed down slid into Southern California." For whatever reasons, it was a lively, happy gathering of many of the people I liked and loved most. Kristin feels the same way about her family, friends and our wedding reception.

My euphoria that day contained other contributing factors. I was marrying Kristin Thorsdale, a beautiful California girl (a blind-date only one year earlier). Her intelligence, contrasting interests, creativity and zest for life were attractive assets that have lasted over 50 years living together. 'Fortunate too, because I think we all marry strangers. And, a marriage is not just a partnership between two people, but a blending of two cultures, presenting many opportunities for things to come unglued.

As my Naval discharge occurred just 48 hours before the wedding, we were also celebrating my re-entry into civilian life. Plans for our immediate future were exciting. We left the wedding reception for a cross-country honeymoon drive in a gifted, new Volvo sedan. I was resigned to not having my Corvette anymore, a favored part of my defunct bachelorhood (a state in which I insisted I had been quite content, but one in which Kristin insisted I was "dying inside"). We had a 2 week hot, humid, mid-July drive to Boston for me to start my residency at The Children's Hospital. Kristin had to find her first job (as a Mills college graduate), and we had to locate a place to live. We found a small, comfortable apartment in the Brighton neighborhood of Boston on Sidlaw Rd. just off Commonwealth Ave. Its kitchen and living room windows looked directly out at the yellow-grey brick expanse of a next door

Jewish Temple, a far cry from the Laguna Beach vistas we had recently left behind. In practically no time, my medical training resumed and Kristin was working in Harvard's Public Health School, next door to Children's Hospital. We were on our way. At no other time for us was the future ever so brimming with a mix of potential opportunity and nervous apprehension.

Over a long marriage there have been many highs. The birth of 2 children and the adoption of 2 others were supremely exciting and fulfilling events. Also some lows (depressions, addictions, and the deaths of our parents, a sibling and our oldest son). The consoling aspect of the highs and the lows has been a sharing of the spectrum of emotions together. Mutual support for the lows was possible because there seems to be a "first law of cohabitation" which dictates that rarely will both partners be down and defeated at the same time or to the same degree.

Beyond that, I never try to analyze marriage too closely.

I do partially subscribe to what Boston Globe columnist Sam Allis once wrote; "… the key to a 50 year marriage is a seamless neurotic fit. A seamless neurotic fit can be anything. All that matters is that the two pathologies occupy sympathetic angles of repose."

Mr. Allis' view may be a bit harsh, but it's not completely off the mark. The important idea is finding 'a seamless fit,' however long that may take and however many iterations 'a fit' may undergo. It seems the major ingredient is commitment to working it out, somehow.

RIVER TRIP

THE COMPANY'S MOTTO WAS 'GO WITH THE FLOW.' The Holiday Rafting Co. brochure described an outdoor adventure idyll; oared, inflatable boats floating down cold canyon rivers, the trip framed by stark, desert scenery and punctuated by daring rides through white-water rapids. I couldn't have predicted that, later in the adventure, I would be tightly hugging one frightened, shivering son while he stuttered; "Why is this happening to us?"

It was a vacation for our family of 6. We rendezvoused in Salt Lake City with 4 other families (7 adults, 10 children in all) for a June run down the Green and Yampa rivers in

Colorado and Utah. Our guides were four, 20-something, strapping river boatmen with fitting back-county names, like Mack, Luke and Sherpa. During an orientation meeting they were enthusiastic and affable, but emphasized that once on the river, we would be in steep walled gorges for the 5 days, lacking all communication with the outside world. We would be taking nature on her conditions, not ours. I began wondering, *is this really how families with kids should vacation?*

Our first few days on the water were so wondrous and

serene we mostly forgot the orientation's foreboding reminders. The weather was clear with a high-desert dry 70 – 80 degrees. The guides made robust campfire meals daily. We slept on mats under starry skies, lulled to sleep by the splashing rumble of nearby swirling currents. Each day we boarded two giant rubber rafts to drift lazily downriver, enjoying each other's company while taking in the frequent wildlife, obscure dark caves, and rock petroglyphs along the riverbanks. Every now and then our tranquility was interrupted by a roaring, boat bending, topsy-turvy adrenalin high as the guides' struggled to navigate class III – IV, boulder strewn whirlpools of white water. We survived those fearsome forays soaked, exhilarated and a bit apprehensive about the next one around the bend.

About the 4th day the script changed dramatically. Morning dark clouds were already forming as we rowed out to join the current. Within an hour the warm desert temperature plunged to the 40's, accompanied by a cold rain that sent all scurrying for sweaters and plastic rain capes (all were unequipped for such severe weather). As the sky turned black, thunder roared as torrential rain and hail drove down, filling the boats and ripping our thin rain gear. Many of the adults, and all of the children, quickly were hypothermic, some showing dangerous symptoms of severe shivering and confusion. Our survival clearly depended on the actions of the boatmen as they frantically rowed for the riverbank. The guides eventually started a flaming brush and log fire, around which we huddled in groups, parents tightly hugging frightened children of all ages. It was then, with my arms wrapped around my adolescent son Ian, that he questioned why this calamity had been our fate. I could only think of one answer: that we had signed up for 5 days away from civilization, and that meant surviving on nature's terms, not ours. It was a stark reminder that in the wild, one had to find a way to get by — to "Go with the flow."

An hour later, as the rain tapered off, the warm fire had restored our bodies' heat and saved us from serious consequences. After changing into dry clothes and getting back on the water, we encountered a spectacular visual reward. The sun had returned, the temperature risen. Hundreds of narrow, towering, rain-bowed waterfalls cascaded down both sides of the canyon as the desert shed the recent deluge. Even the amazed, perpetually laconic boatmen began shouting, "Can you believe this?"

Rivers and river trips are often metaphors for life. Nevertheless, that wild river experience was a great lesson in my life, one that I have relied upon many times in the years since. When things are going badly and I'm under duress, the aphorism that always comes to mind...and soothes my soul...is the rafters' motto: 'Go with the flow'.

Postscript: A 2017 memoir, *"Disaster Falls, A Family Story"* by S. Gerson describes a couple's search for acceptance after their 8-year-old son's accidental death on a white-water rafting trip — eerily, down the same Green River our trip took.

One morning on a group guided river float, inexperienced Gerson decided to take his son in a light, inflatable rubber kayak known as a 'ducky,' through a white-water rapid named "Disaster Falls." The guides didn't dissuade him, despite the ducky being less stable than the group's large rafts. Gerson let the kayak get too close to some rocks where it flipped, sucking the 2 underwater. The father broke free but his son Owen was caught in rocks and drowned. The book details the heart-rending efforts of the couple to deal with the immediate horror of event, its long-term effects on their psyche, and the eventual ways they assuaged their remorse. I can't imagine how I might have coped with such a tragedy.

And there's good reason for me to think about it. Starting out one morning during our family's trip down the Yampa and Green Rivers, our youngest child Jesse, then 10, was pleading to paddle one of the 'duckies' some of our group's older boys were taking downstream that day. I explained to him that there would be waterfalls and dangerous rapids along the way, and that he was too young to risk it. "If they're crazy enough to do it, let them," I insisted. He responded; "Dad, I am crazy enough." I loved the humor in his reasoning, but not the logic. I refused permission. The long-term outcome was a good river story and a loving son now grown into a delightful adult...with no dark event to mark the memories of our family rafting adventure.

DAD

THE BEGINNING OF THE END. Coasting to a stop in the retirement home parking lot, we are a somber, melancholy group — 3 middle-aged brothers delivering our 82-year-old, confused and questioning father to the last station on his life's journey.

He is a frail image of his former vigorous self, his wavy black hair gone wispy grey, his stout body now thin, his chest sunken and his eyes colorless. Only his signature Bay Rum aftershave smell, still there, to remind us of who he once was. Not relishing the task at hand, we are doing it for our distraught mother whose 52 year married life has become unmanageable supporting a cranky, forgetful and demanding spouse for the past 6 years.

Our reluctance to initiate this final chapter was compounded by our guilt: we were transporting him under a false premise — "to check out a new apartment." He actually managed a smile and some enthusiasm as we entered the retirement home's lobby. That momentary lift in his spirit was squashed minutes later when we entered a windowless, crowded, twin-bedded room. There, an elderly male 'roommate' watched warily from his chair as we mumbled, "Dad, you're going to stay here now. This is your new home."

Try as I may, I can't recall his whole reaction. I've blocked it out. I do remember his bewildered expression sitting tentatively at the edge of his bed. He protested his fate, "Please don't do this to me." But, did he cry? Did he moan? Did he just give in, give up, defeated and resigned? I know I was sad, about to cry myself, and anxious to drop his suitcases and flee as rapidly as possible. The drive home and the rest of that day are also a blank page for me.

My Dad and namesake, Kenneth E. Fellows, was an earnest, virtuous Midwesterner, a loyal, loving husband, an attentive, generous father and a caring, successful physician.

The only child of working class, intelligent parents he was a self-made man. Defying considerable family pressure to be a professional violinist, he funded his own medical education working dangerous nights in a train yard checking boxcars. Having no role-model, he apparently was 'a medical natural' — empathetic, comfortable with all sorts of people, knowledgeable and effective. He began as a family doctor during The Depression and then became a radiologist who created a busy private office practice for both diagnostic x-ray studies and radiation therapy for cancer patients. He sometimes took me on house calls when his cancer patients needed attention for pain or dressing changes: they called him, preferring his care to that of their own family physician. I suspect they noticed and liked his hands: large but soft, meaty and velvet smooth. Healing hands.

My father and I had a loving relationship that could flare volatile in brief instances of our competing strong wills. In my early 20's our most serious clash arose — briefly but bitterly — in a flurry of punches over some ill chosen words by both of us. Most of my memories are happy: annual spring fishing trips on Michigan's Little Manistee River, his summertime joy driving the boat while pulling water skis, and our playing endless hours of baseball catch after dinner at home. He was highly concerned about my welfare and always ready with advice, even when I didn't want it: "No, you can't play tackle football. It's too dangerous." As it turned out he probably prevented a number of boyhood head, knee or other injuries for me. Fortunately, even our biggest disagreement worked itself out. He was intent on my joining his private practice of radiology, while I was similarly emphatic about carving my own career in academia. My will prevailed. He not only came to accept my choice, but ultimately was proud of my accomplishments as an academic Pediatric Radiologist.

Revisiting my Dad in the retirement home, I bring my son Ian, 7. I want the 3 generations together for possibly a last time. With some help from me, Ian pushes my bent-over, head-in-hands father in a wheel chair through the bland, faintly urine smelling corridors. My father seems to know me but not my name; he has no idea who his grandson is. The image of my father that day — a frail, despondent, mostly silent, grey ghost of himself — depresses me. I acknowledge to myself then, this is it: dad's last days are close.

When dementia overtakes a loved one there is a human tendency to keep looking for "the real person inside." Not me. I believe "memory is identity" (Julian Barnes). We are only our thoughts — the ideas arising in our minds. I have no belief in a 'me' somewhere deep inside — no clandestine "cerebral submarine captain of the ship" (JB) ultimately in charge. When the relevant thoughts are gone, so is the person. Then, so was my father.

As often happens, he died silently one night, after

just a few months in the home. His former friend and colleague, Dr. Fred Brace, listed the cause of death as "lung congestion", a perfunctory diagnosis at best. It was from a final station named Dementia that he departed for eternity. He died alone and without recourse, which may have been inevitable, but I still wonder if we might not have done better, somehow? Do parents ever die without leaving family feeling some guilt?

I delivered the eulogy at his funeral. It was my final wave goodbye. If I had been able to speak to him on his deathbed, knowing what I do know about dying well, I would have included four time honored 'closings:' "I forgive you." "Please forgive me." "Thank you." "I love you."

BROTHER RICK

I SLOWLY REPLACED THE BEDROOM PHONE, stunned by the news that my 35 year old bachelor brother Rick had hanged himself. My brother John, who discovered his body, called from Toledo, Ohio with the news. Always the loyal, caring, responsible one, John had done all the things that needed doing — 'called the police, talked to the coroner, gathered up the suicide note and packed up Rick's few valuables. I promised him I'd fly out to Michigan as soon as possible.

Richard Fellows (Rick to most) was an affable young man well suited to his work as a bartender and radio advertising salesman. But, he practiced a reclusive life, living in a sparsely furnished apartment in a rundown part of Toledo, a lackluster Midwestern town. He didn't earn very much but got by with some periodic subsidies from our mother. She and my 2 other siblings lived in Michigan, 100 miles from Toledo, but they were never invited to visit him, and only infrequently did he visit them.

Living in the suburbs of Philadelphia, my contact with Rick was limited to 1 or 2 phone calls each year. I initiated those calls except for the last one a month before his death, when surprisingly, he called me. I should have been suspicious something was up, but he sounded upbeat and I was happy for his seeking a conversation. We'd never been very close. Of the 4 children, I was the oldest, Rick the youngest —16 years younger than I. His conception had been unplanned. Separated from his other siblings by at least 10 years, he always felt his life was an accident, his existence some mistake.

Rick was a curious guy, a non-linear thinker for sure. He was tall and thin, a handsome clothes-horse who struggled to afford his stylish wardrobe. His IQ was very high, his imagination broad, and his reality-testing low. He fancied himself an intellect, a gourmet chef, an amateur boxer and an adventurer perpetually headed on archeological expeditions that never materialized. He was a firm believer in the lost city of Atlantis, seers like Nostradamus and other mystical ideas. Lurking behind all of this was an incurable, isolating disease: alcoholism. It was not until we talked to several of his longtime friends in Michigan and Ohio that we pieced together his 20 year history of progressive, excessive drinking. A poignant part of his suicide note, left under a bottle of bourbon, read; "...AA hasn't helped, religion doesn't work, I'm out of options. Please forgive me, Mom."

Several days after John's call we were together in Rick's dilapidated apartment, salvaging a few things and throwing out most of his possessions. We took down from a living room wall a black and white, photo portrait of our father, the parent with whom Rick had a long, tumultuous relationship: my father was a pragmatist, Rick a dreamer. John whispered to me that he had found Rick hanging...right in front of our Dad's picture. That detail made Rick's death even more sad.

I should have been better prepared for this suicide

—it wasn't the first in our family. My mother-in-law, also afflicted by alcoholism, already had taken her life by overdosing on pills. Instead of new stress and grief reactions, I was reliving old ones: some despair and sadness, considerable anger and resentment. The overwhelming effect of a suicide is that it always leaves family members and friends 'holding the bag' — asking over and over "why didn't we notice something?.... why didn't we call more, talk more often, show more compassion?...what could we have done to prevent this?" Those thoughts can persist like an interminable echo.

The oldest of my own four children, Ian, was an especially bright young man who understood Rick, his favorite uncle, better than others in the family I think. When it became apparent that Ian too was afflicted by alcoholism, I often worried that their lives might have a parallel path. And they did. Ian died unexpectedly at age 37 of heart disease, to some degree complicated by his addictions. At least, not another suicide.

Tragically it was again brother John who, living in Grand Rapids — as did Ian — discovered him dead on the floor of his apartment. Again he had to call me with devastating news. My first reaction on that hot July evening was, after calmly telling Kristin that Ian was dead, to step outside to send a long, primordial scream into the darkening sky. The grief that developed — a heavy, grey curtain drawn over every day and every event, indistinguishable from clinical depression — was much greater than after Rick's death and, in its cyclical, recurrent nature, much more prolonged.

Some find comfort in the philosophical (religious?) myth; "God never gives people more than they can handle." I find it the most stupid, maddening thought ever offered to those who are suffering. Personally there's no part of it that makes sense.

"Who bent the coin of my destiny that it sticks in the slot...?" mused Patrick Kavanagh in his story "The Hunger." I prefer this poetic way of contemplating my concerns about our family legacy of tragic deaths — and any karmic affect on us and our progeny.

MISSING

OUR FAMILY MOVED TO THE PHILADELPHIA SUBURBS in1987. On a warm October evening we were gathering for dinner when we noticed Maria, our 17 year old daughter, was missing.

"Oh no, she did it!" her 15-year-old sister Hannah gasped.

"Did what?"

"Ran away," she mumbled, tearing.

Maria had told Hannah the day before that she was having "running away fantasies." This was troubling news. This had been a coping device for Maria as a child in Columbia. Adopted there as a baby and abused by her Columbian stepmother, she put herself back on a bus to the orphanage at age 6. Adopted by us at 8, she sometimes said that when stressed she often felt like "just running away again." And she was stressed. We had just moved from Newton, MA to Rose Valley, PA, forcing her to make new friends and other difficult changes.

"Where'd she go?" I asked Hannah.

"Don't know," she whispered.

I felt startled and sickened. I presumed she had run

off using the nearby commuter train. Dire alternatives stirred in my head also—abduction, suicide, murder? Frantic calls to neighbors and Maria's friends revealed only that, absent from school that day, she hadn't been seen by anyone.

We called the police and within minutes I was in a scene I had always feared: sitting in my house with a uniformed PA State policeman, describing the facts of my child's disappearance. His reassurance —"most of these kids show up in few days" —was well intended, but not at all comforting.

When I was 8 or 9 I had already decided that having children was way too risky. I spent most of my time then in a large, public park and I saw what could happen. Kids got lost and injured; ran away, or were kidnapped. The loss would be unbearable. 'Better not to become a parent, ever.

Of course, I did become a parent. Kristin and I had 4 children; Ian and Hannah birthed, and then Jesse and Maria adopted. I never expected raising children would be a cakewalk, but I also never thought my childhood anxieties would actually materialize.

The next day, searching for clues, I found a scrap of paper in our family trash in Maria's handwriting. It read: "to New York City." That was our only lead.

I could barely work, eat or sleep over the next few days. Struggling, I finally decided to take leave of my hospital responsibilities to begin doing something... anything...to relieve my distress and, I hoped, find Maria. Without a better clue or much of a plan, I headed for New York City.

Checking into my NYC hotel I felt a sudden surge of engagement, even a hint of exhilaration. I was on a mission and there was some giddy energy in that, as well as some relief from my panic. I headed straight for Times Square, assuming runaways would congregate at that bustling crossroads, a fact confirmed by the first burly NY cop I encountered. He recommended I begin my search at Covenant House, a large, nonprofit refuge for runaways, nearby on 9th Ave.

My hope for news from that sanctuary disappeared at the front desk. Their protective policy forbade divulging the names of, or any information about, the adolescents sheltered there. I was invited to leave a short message in case Maria showed up. Then, for the better part of the following 2 days, I walked the streets of Manhattan, hoping for a miracle — a chance encounter perhaps. It never happened.

Deflated, I returned to Philly. Each morning and evening Kristin and I hugged and cried together, trying otherwise to resume our lives as best we could. Kristin, fearing Maria's suicide, still periodically searched the neighborhood for her body.

Midafternoon, one week after Maria's disappearance, Kristin phoned. Maria had just called from a Bronx Police Station confessing in a weak, child-like voice that she had run away and now wanted us to come get her. What wondrous news it was, but curiously anticlimactic too. Why was I so calm? Had I become addicted to the adrenalin surge?

That evening Kristin and I drove to the Bronx under a remarkably clear, starry sky. Even the lights of NYC had a pristine glow, contrasting starkly with the dark, grim of the S. Bronx Station House. The Desk Sergeant directed us to Maria in a small anteroom where she sat smiling faintly, looking awkward and embarrassed. Across the room, hand-cuffed to a radiator, a glum, teenage boy bore sad witness to the hugs and kisses of our joyful, but awkward, reunion.

We drove back to Philly that night not discussing the incident and its attendant turmoil. Maria ever after has been reluctant to divulge many details. We did learn she had been sheltered by someone in Times Square much of the time. At least my frantic mid-Manhattan search had been "close."

Another crisis involving Maria occurred a few years later, not a disappearance but another stressful family incident. Those experiences, worrying and wearing as they were, helped Maria and us eventually forge a stronger, loving relationship. In the process, she learned a lot about honesty, and we about acceptance.

Being a survivor, Maria finished high school and graduated from Smith College. Eventually she attained postgraduate degrees in Writing and then Social Work. In her professional family-counseling practice she now brings her deep understanding of adolescent impulses and behaviors to the families and young adults she cares for there.

She's also written a memoir of her early struggles in life, her star-crossed, successful search to find her Columbian birth mother, and her resilient success in surviving a mountain of personal obstacles. A great story to be published "sometime," it is gathering 'shelf-time' — maturing and mellowing like a good wine.

SNAPSHOT

THE PHOTO: That's my 37-year-old son Ian and I, July 4, 2006, talking after breakfast while a hot summer's day unfolds over the harbor islands in Stonington, one of my favorite places in Maine.

WHAT I SEE: The father and son have come to accept and enjoy one another despite a considerable age gap, adult connection limited mostly to telephone calls and holiday visits, and several basic differences in what constitutes a fulfilling life.

The relaxed, hands-in-lap parent is listening to a tense, possibly ill, son who is anxious to discuss some of his worries and despair, but not all.

CONTEXT: July 2nd was our 40th wedding anniversary, and we were celebrating by gathering our 4 adult children (with spouses and partners) together in a large Stonington Harbor rental. Everyone was in a calm, celebratory mood except Ian. He had recently parted with his girlfriend of several years in Grand Rapids (MI), was now living alone there, and was generally upset by personal and businesses stresses in his life. The positive parts of his conversation described his serious search for

better values in life, less materialism, and an expanded spirituality in his future.

ASSOCIATIONS: I was uneasy sitting with Ian that morning. I was trying hard to be a good listener because he seemed to need one, but I was distracted by his vulnerability and how different he was from the confident person he had been.

I was remembering a highly energetic youngster, generous with hugs and loving pats, precociously clever in conversation and confident in his sense of style: he declared around age 6 while riding in the family's old 4-door sedan; "Dad, I don't think I look very good in this car!"

He had grown into a boisterous, engaging entrepreneur, using his considerable intellect and robust sense of humor to build a successful career in medical devices. He dazzled family and friends with encyclopedic knowledge (built over years by voracious reading and a photographic memory), and entertained to tears with his funny stories, impersonations and witty observations. Terry Jones of the Monty Python Flying Circus was Ian's accidental but close English friend for several years. He described Ian as one of his "funniest and smartest friends."

Ian had a dominating presence in our family circle, where he often seemed to occupy the space of 2 or 3 people, exasperating his siblings and confounding his parents. That part of him was missing at our anniversary party.

Instead, sitting and talking to me was a distraught, middle-aged son who had lost his swagger. He was most concerned about his businesses and a considerable sum of money he needed to find before serious legal problems arose. For good reasons, his affect and his thinking had the aura of a major midlife crisis.

Most uncharacteristically, his trademark sense of humor was missing. He complained that most events now seemed mostly sad, not funny. In retrospect, there were indications of impending trouble some months before. When I had asked him if some of the events in his life were affecting his equanimity, he responded with typical irony; "No, but I'm maintaining my serenity with a new, low level of anger."

Several days following this photo the family reunion ended. As everyone was leaving for home (New England, Pennsylvania, Michigan, California), Ian's mother and his sister Hannah remarked that his good-bye hugs seemed unusually intent.

Just 2 weeks later we all unexpectedly and hastily reconvened in Grand Rapids. Ian had died suddenly, prematurely and tragically from unrecognized heart disease. We came together again as a family, this time to grieve, arrange his cremation and settle his affairs. Now, for all of us, he would always be 37 years old and never change from our keepsake Stonington pictures.

Whenever I look at this picture of Ian Edward Fellows and me, I recall this quote I used in his memorial service; "…all of us live by forces we only pretend to understand" (WH Auden). And these lines from Edna St. Vincent Millay…

  My candle burns at both ends, it will not last the night
But ah my foes, an oh my friends, it gives a lovely light

Parental love is forever.

IAN EDWARD FELLOWS RECOLLECTIONS

His life

Ian Edward Fellows was born on a crisp December 16th day, 1968, in Ann Arbor, Michigan. He was the first of what eventually would be 4 children (Maria, Hannah, and Jesse the others) for Kristin and Ken Fellows. It was a memorable day; a family begun.

Growing up in Newton, Massachusetts, Ian was a handsome, lovable boy with an engaging personality. His Aunt Jane described his demeanor as that of "a little prince". He precociously developed lofty ideas quite early on. When 6 or 7, while leaving for an errand in the family's old Volvo sedan, he turned to his father; "You know Dad, I don't think I look very good in this car." There were long-term implications of that statement.

My fond recollection of his childhood was what a loving little boy he was. He was always liberal with hugs and little pats on the back, references to which sometimes appeared on his grade school report cards, his appreciative teachers lacking other substantive good things to say about a hyperactive, distractible boy.

2

His considerable intellect was evident in childhood, although it never manifested itself in superior academic achievement in grade school, high school or college. In later life, his photographic memory and speed-reading abilities created an extensive and facile knowledge with which he could be dazzling, overbearing, or sometimes both.

Ian was generally precocious about expressing himself and his feelings. While attending a Harvard - Cornell hockey game (while a 6th grade goalie himself), he was asked by his pushy father if he could see himself one day playing at the college level; his response was; "No, Dad. You know I don't tolerate pain very well."

In late childhood his devious sense of humor became evident; he could turn almost any event or happening into a funny story. He loved to do Marx brothers' bits with his dad, and could recite long sections of any sketch from Monty Python movies or TV programs. Later in life he acquired the ability to mimic most dialects and foreign accents, which further enhanced his comedic skills.

The transition from childhood to adolescence didn't go easily for Ian. Although he found much to be enthusiastic about, some darker levels in his life began to form. The melancholic side of his personality emerged, along with an affinity for mood altering substances (starting with pot). Neither he nor his parents knew then that the family disease of alcoholism was about to afflict another. Despite these problems and distractions, he not only finished Newton North High School, but he went on to graduate (with a degree in Fine Art) from Dickinson College in Pennsylvania. Reflecting later, on his years at Dickinson, he said that all the academic and social problems he encountered there were self-inflicted, and alcohol related. Those years were further complicated by 2 kidney operations (for a congenital defect) and a long convalescence. The associated pain and morbidity (reflected in a 'sutured sculpture' he made) affected him considerably, but he persevered.

3

One of Ian's first summer jobs while in college was assisting in cardiovascular imaging research at the precursor company for Boston Scientific. His exposure there to the business world led him to conclude; "Don't trust what salesmen say: they lie." His early introduction there into the development of devices for the diagnosis and treatment of heart disease, along with experience during several subsequent summers working in the cardiac catheterization labs at Children's Hospital (Boston), firmly determined his life's work and career path.

His first job was promotion and sales with a company in Minnesota making innovative guidewires for vascular and cardiac catheterization. After several years on the road in New England and the midwest, he joined Cardia, INC., a startup company which had developed (with input from Ian) a catheter-deliverable device for closing congenital holes in human hearts. He spent 4-5 years, mostly in Europe, introducing this device to European cardiologists and working with them in their hospitals, teaching them how to implant this "umbrella" through catheters into the heart.

When not working, the intellectual side of him reveled in the European history so close at hand; the grand cathedrals, art museums, and architectural marvels all around him. He also had opportunities for travel beyond Europe to Israel and the middle East. For a young, unmarried man he was living a stimulating and fulfilling life.

4

That life, full of excitement, travel and new friends was his delight for several years, but it became increasingly burdensome, and the isolation and stress began to enhance the depressive side of his personality. Also, the disease of alcoholism (which he later said he admitted only to himself) was progressing.

During those early years of his business career there were romantic interludes with women in both the United States and Europe; most were intense but short-lived relationships. His good friends Michel and Gabriella Willi in Zurich named him the godfather of their first child, Carolina, an honor that made him proud and happy. He loved Carolina as if she were his own child.

He finally came to loathe his life on the road, running from one European city to another. He abruptly quit Cardia and sold his company stock. He came home to Kittery Point briefly to get his bearings and look for a new job. Through a series of events over some months, the most significant being a severe auto accident (a demolished Porsche without no personal injury), he "hit bottom" and agreed to enter an alcohol rehabilitation program. He was embarrassed to have caused his parents so much distress, contrite and humbled; perhaps for the first time in his life he began to realize that his superior intelligence and confident brashness were not enough to carry him in this world.

That rude awakening and new insight allowed him to gain a renewal of his confidence and an improved outlook from the 12-step rehab program he successfully completed in February 2002. However, that 12-step progress came with a warning from his counselors; they worried that Ian was so smart that he would tend to think and act more like an addiction therapist than a patient in need. To considerable extent, that eventually happened.

He went directly from the rehab center in Pennsylvania to Grand Rapids, correctly thinking that his girlfriend Elizabeth and his loyal uncle John Fellows could provide the best support for his new sobriety. He went there to start a new life in recovery.

He actually began that new life modestly in Grand Rapids, painting houses by day and attending meetings each evening. However, within the first few months family relationships became strained after his hiring some relatives (also afflicted with the family disease of addiction) caused work financial problems. A rift soon developed between Ian, a cousin, an Aunt and others.

Despite that rocky beginning, Ian's active imagination and entrepreneurial nature were already engaged in beginning what would eventually become 4 new businesses, each featuring new ideas and products for dentistry and medicine. Conceptualizing and coaxing these enterprises into existence were the largest achievements of his life, and produced some happy and fulfilling years.

At the same time, as managing his businesses became more stressful, his recovery and associated equanimity diminished. When I observed then that his serenity seemed less, he countered; "No, I still have my serenity, but I'm maintaining it with a low level of anger." That quip was both funny and prophetic.

5

In early 2006 venture capital funding for the largest of his projects (InfoMD, of which he was president) was withdrawn. As his office staff dwindled and his stress increased, his enthusiasm was gradually supplanted by worry and depression. He mentioned in July that year that this descent into melancholy actually began before his business problems, with the breakup of his long relationship with Elizabeth in early spring of 2006.

The late spring of 2006 was the most tormented period of his life. Depression was unrelenting and punctuated with bouts of anxiety and panic. Fortunately, he regularly sought medical and psychological counseling throughout this time, and managed to block the disease of alcoholism from again taking over his life. By June, however, it was taking a considerable amount of prescription sleep medication for him to find rest at night, and the hangover from that medication during the day began to affect his memory and other functioning (a phenomenon now referred to in psychiatry as the "Patrick Kennedy Syndrome").

Ian Edward Fellows died unexpectedly, in the afternoon or evening of July 22, 2006. He was found by his uncle John the next day on his living room floor, the TV on and his dog Dingo beside him. A coroner's autopsy discovered an enlarged (dilated) heart caused by a disease of the heart muscle (a cardiomyopathy). The presumed cause of death was an electrical disturbance (a cardiac arrhythmia, likely ventricular fibrillation), a lethal complication occurring in abnormal hearts.

7
Reflecting on Ian's Life

Just 2 weeks before his death, Ian's parents had the good fortune to celebrate their 40th wedding anniversary over several days with all their children at a house rented for the occasion in Stonington, Maine. Although his psychological distress was overt and disturbing, other aspects of his life and thinking (about which we had no idea) came to light. He really was at a crossroad in his personal philosophy, what he suspected was a "mid-life crisis". He described how, in the past year, his spiritual development had become a priority, and (among other things) he had found inspiration in the sermons he heard at Fountain St. Church in Grand Rapids. Simultaneously, he was rejecting the materialism that had seemed so important during his formative years: he was proud of his new, modest apartment, and becoming embarrassed by the expensive car he was still driving. One of the best outcomes of his time with the family was his making amends with his sister Hannah on the last day they were together. He even called her after his return to Grand Rapids to congratulate her on her maturity and to tell her he loved her. He also wrote a thank-you note to his parents concluding it with an expression of his abiding love for them. Although depressed, anxious and lonely, he was not defeated and seemed to be reaching out to those he cared about most.

On July 25th, most of his immediate family gathered in Grand Rapids to get Ian's affairs in order and to arrange for his cremation. Over 4 sorrowful days we learned even more about his life in the Michigan. His struggle to control his anxiety and depression was illustrated by numerous recently purchased self-help books and CDs on those subjects. There were color photos on his desk of Asian children he had recently sponsored through an international charity. The most compelling evidence of his search for redemption and continued recovery was an outline he wrote for making amends with his estranged cousins. This was particularly gratifying to his uncle John Fellows who had been discussing such a plan with Ian for some time. Finally, at the end of that difficult week in Grand Rapids, when nearly all Fellows' family members got together, there was ambient love and goodwill despite the grief. Also, some other signs that the legacy of Ian's untimely death might be further reconciliation among his estranged Grand Rapids relatives. Others have observed that in our grief, we find ways to ease our pain and discomfort.

Final Thoughts

Buddhists often liken the fragility of life to a flickering candle flame in a gusting wind. Ian's life more resembled a sparkler lit in a stormy gale. His appetites were huge, his expectations high, his enthusiasm great, his intellect superior, his sense of humor memorable, his ideas original, and his physical presence imposing. He could light up a gathering with his wit, or deflate a group with his sarcasm. Whatever he was offering came full-force. Whenever he came home to visit as an adult, it felt as if at least 2 personalities had arrived, telling stories, making jokes, asking provocative questions and describing volumes of books, articles and ideas he had read or heard about. His death leaves a giant intellectual and entertainment hole in our lives.

From his recovery program he knew his character defects, and just as he seemed ready to address them, his time ran out. His afflicted soul is at rest now; he finally has an abiding peace that his life could not provide.

We who will forever hold fast his fond memory will always remember the sparkling personality and brilliant individual who was our dear Ian.

Ken Fellows
Kittery Pt., Maine
August 14, 2006

POST SCRIPT: The Monty Python Flying Circus was Ian's favorite comic group. When in his mid-20's he chanced to meet Terry Jones, an original Python member, and they became fast-friends. Ian often stayed with Terry and his family when in London, where at Python parties Ian entertained by reciting their own material (in perfect dialect) for them. Ian also coached Terry through serious health problems. Terry Jones appealed to Ian because he was an intellectual and a highly educated man. It was weeks after Ian's death that Terry found out and wrote; "Ian was a funny, smart man."

BEING A GRANDFATHER

I HAVE GREAT MEMORIES of my grandfather, 'Gene' Fellows. He possessed only an 8th grade education but eventually became the head electrical engineer for a large Grand Rapids furniture factory. He read history extensively, making himself an authority on Abraham Lincoln and the Roman Empire. His thorough knowledge of contemporary national and international affairs caused me problems; I always did poorly on his frequent, spontaneous quizzes.

He was a wiry, thin man with sparse, short grey hair, bright blue eyes, and a prominent nose. He smoked a straight stemmed pipe and smelled of Prince Albert tobacco. Most of my childhood he lived on a small, vegetable farm on the outskirts of Grand Rapids, Michigan. When I was 5 or 6 I lived there for 6 months during WWII. Recalling that time, his own tobacco smell and the fragrance of corn fields and strawberry patches are strong in my memory.

My grandfather doted on me because we were often together during the time my father was an Army Medical Officer in France. My 3 siblings never benefited as much from his knowledge or received as much of his attention. He was a skilled tradesman and a stern taskmaster prone to profane exclamations when observing my boyhood work ethic. His expectations were usually higher than I could deliver, producing in me a third-generation perfectionist who had a youthful command of a precociously colorful vocabulary. As a small kid, I sometimes shocked nearby adults and children with an emphatic "God-Damn-It" or 'Jesus-H-Christ" when alarmed or angry.

My grandfather also had a lighter side, often singing to me children's songs and folk tunes and occasionally dancing a little jig he'd make up and entice me to mimic. From his early railroading years, he was an inveterate card-shark, a skill I never mastered despite his intense instruction. He was also an avowed tea-totaler, explaining he had seen too many railroad men and families ruined by alcohol. It was a personal rule he didn't force on others.

In between history lessons on the Roman Empire and President Lincoln, he mostly struggled to teach me practical skills. A short list of the things I learned from him would include how to drive nails, saw wood, handle most tools (for me he made a red and blue, fully furnished tool chest which still sits on my work bench), how to grow and pick strawberries and sweet corn, how to paint a house filling every crack and covering every nail completely, how to coax a recalcitrant 2 cycle engine to start, and how to maintain motors and mechanical devices to last 100 years. He took me fishing in rowboats on small lakes and off long Lake Michigan stone piers, ones with a defining one story red brick lighthouse at their seaward end. We fished with long bamboo poles baited with minnows for lake perch and white fish which we kept in a bucket of lake water or on a stringer tied to the pier. Those captive fish in their varying states of demise were endlessly fascinating.

My fondest grandfatherly memory arises from the

many times I curled in his lap before dinner, while he in his big, thickly padded, red leather rocker, tuned the living room radio to the day's news (the Texaco news-hour; H.C. Keltenborn, announcer), and again after dinner when he lit up his pipe and we sang "The Bear Went Over the Mountain," "Go Tell Aunt Roady," and others in the same chair. On the floor next to that big rocker was a shiny brass spittoon and a dark cherry ash-tray-stand holding boxes of wooden matches, his red Prince Albert can and several old pipes at the ready.

My grandfather never spoke about love or affection that I recall. In those days, such emotions were mostly implied, not often verbalized. Excepting that quirk, I realize now he was constantly imprinting on me an important life's lesson; how to be a good grandfather.

STRAWBERRIES AND GRANDPARENTS

THE TASTE OF A GOOD STRAWBERRY SHORTCAKE always reminds me of my 1940's childhood. I spent many days back then harvesting strawberries with my grandparents on their small farm in Michigan. The evocative smells and sounds from the from those good times still echo strongly some 70 years later.

My grandmother Jesse Fellows—a round, gingham-aproned woman with short grey hair, redundant upper arm skin and low-rider "spectacles" —smelled of hard-boiled, naphtha soaked house dresses and antique closet mustiness. She often spoke to me (and her uncontrollable pet Boxer) in an extreme falsetto, exclaiming "oh my dosh!" and other homey non-sequiturs. She occasionally admitted to getting messages from "little people" perched on her shoulders.

Her old blue Dodge sedan, its seats smoothly covered by hand-stitched, faded flannel sheets, smelled a lot like her, but with added chrome polish and glass cleaner overtones.

That beloved clunker could "still get out and dust" she liked to remind people.

Eugene Fellows, my grandfather, was wiry, energetic

and intense. He was bathed once a week, and his grey hair brush-cut monthly, by my grandmother. His clothes were hard-boiled plain and clean like hers, but he smelled sweetly of Prince Albert tobacco ("in the red can," a perfect fit in his shirt pocket), and wispy pipe-smoke. When I sat in his lap after lunch or dinner — for a mandatory digestive pause — he would sing "The Bear Went Over the Mountain" and other kid's songs, the smell of his big leather rocker blending perfectly with the tobacco aromas. The raspy scratch of matches struck against his pipe stand, followed by the sulfurous burst of the match flames were accents to those fond times.

Grandpa's professional-grade, basement workbench smelled of old wooden tools, sawdust, and electric-motor ozone, all slightly modified by coalbin dust. As much time as I spent making things with him there, it was his gardening — especially his huge strawberry patch — that is most memorable. I helped my grandparents pick, sort and store scores of strawberries when I was between the ages of 6 and 12. Even a faint whiff of contemporary, half-ripe, supermarket berries takes me back to kneeling in the dirt, picking hot fields on June summer days — and hearing the distinctive "pop" of plump, red berries plucked from the vines. Sixteen thin-wooden quart boxes were packed in lightweight wooden crates, dozens of which were hauled off each year to a farm shed for sorting the fruit by size and quality. Then, intense discussions followed between my grandparents on how to divide and distribute the barter: strawberries were the currency they used to pay for their medical care, dental work and other professional services.

Dinner those evenings was commonly just a dinner-plate sized strawberry shortcake for each of us, made with round, thick soda biscuits and topped with juicy red berries and thick whipped-cream.

I had no idea, of course, that I was experiencing something then that would never be the same. Occasionally I get good, local strawberries now — ironically from a carpenter friend who also is a great gardener — good enough to approximate the taste and aroma of those shortcakes in my past. Distressingly, I sometimes find myself at the local Dairy Queen ordering a strawberry sundae for my granddaughter Ella, a treat she finds delightful but I know is a far cry from the real thing. I wish I had a time machine so I could take her back to the pure taste of berries unadulterated by fructose syrups and chemical enhancers. And then, maybe as an adult she too will be wistful about these DQ treats of her youth, when describing all the things that were better in her "back then."

I'M A GRANDPA

I'M NOW 73 AND SMITTEN by my 3-year-old grand-daughter, Ella. Being a grandfather is the most stimulating and pleasurable part of my life. Since her birth I have been captivated by her existence and the joy she brings everyone in our family. Borrowing some street vernacular, "I sure didn't see it coming." It has been so engrossing I've spent considerable time just contemplating how it happened... and why is being a grandpa so good?

A big reason for this late life revelation is Ella's remarkable, extroverted personality. As a father of 4 and a former pediatric specialist, I think I have a pretty good feel for the spectrum of children's personalities; shy or bold, dull or clever, distracted or aware. Ella is such an engaging individual. She's lively, loquacious, humorous and highly self-confident. One evening when she was two I became vocal about her twirling near a glass table: she stopped when I hollered, turned in my direction, and with a firm, both-hands-pushing-down gesture, told me to "calm down Grandpa, just calm down!" Another time, when asked what she thought of a surprise toy gift she offered; "it's fucking gorgeous." When her shocked mother told her, she had just uttered a naughty word, she countered; "no it's not, it's a funny word. Just forget about it!"

Intentional or not, her humorous statements are often good comedy. When I inquired during a game what she meant by "aw shucks", she explained that "shucks is Spanish for bummer." My son Ian and I used to compete for who could be funniest at the dinner table. Ella could have joined in that competition.

Being Ella's grandpa is a golden second chance at life's biggest challenge; to help raise children successfully, or, well enough. It's another time around for me, but with less stress and lower stakes since the primary responsibility lies elsewhere. Because I have more time and experience, I can now exercise the patience I should have had with my own kids, or at least to refine the patience I (should) already possess ("calm down Grandpa, just calm down" echoes in my mind).

Between parenthood and grandparenthood, I've gained insight from many sources, even my brother-in-law. When his children were young he became worried he was yelling too often at his 3 kids, "just like you" (meaning me!). Being a Buddhist, he sought advice from his Guru, who confided, "Go ahead and holler at them, kids love drama. Just don't own the anger!" That's terrific insight, I think. And a great challenge. I'm looking for progress here, not perfection.

Since the death of Ian at age 37 I am acutely aware of the fragility of life. All of our loved ones' experiences are significant and they need to be observed attentively and appreciated fully. So that is what I am trying to do as a grandfather; observe, enjoy and remember..... Ella's wonder at a handful of dandelions or her fascination with Lego pieces on the kitchen floor is as great as a Christmas morning or a visit to the circus. We enjoy our trips to Boston together, often stroll in the woods, and share scary amusement park rides. But best of all is bedtime snuggling while reading her favorite books. It's hard to imagine anything better than that.

Like me, I hope Ella will have good recollections of her Grandfather.

ONE BEST FRIEND

NORMAN AND ELLIE MOSCOW LIVE IN BERKELEY but fly twice each summer to their summer cottage in Bayside (ME), near Belfast. They usually stop in Kittery for an overnight on those long trips. Kristin and I make it to California every year or two. We see each other at least annually, sometimes more.

Norman and I were born and raised in Michigan. He attended Mumford High in Detroit; I, Ottawa Hills High in Grand Rapids . We didn't meet until 1960 when we were students at the U. of Michigan medical school; he was a freshman and I a sophomore. Our long friendship really developed some years later, after we both were married when we reunited in a 1967 Radiology residency back in Ann Arbor. I can't remember how or why things clicked just then. We became good friends so quickly that on December 16, 1968 Norman arrived at University Hospital to see our newborn Ian only minutes after I did. And his heartbreak and grief were about equal to mine when Ian died suddenly at 37 in 2006.

Norman and Ellie had no children themselves, but revelled in a huge extended family in which there were many children whom they loved and nourished. In turn, they treated our children as part of their extended family, mixing our children's pictures on their refrigerator door along with all the others. To our kids, Norman was their adopted Uncle, affectionately called "Greenman" by them for the hue of the shirts he usually wore. They flocked around his car when it pulled into our driveway for another annual visit, excited to see what silly toy—like a paddle/attached rubber-ball 'flyback'—he would exit playing, or what other antic might be sprung on them.

I cherish him as a friend because his major interests, ideas on what matters in life, and sense of humor are parallel to mine. The fact we're both radiologists helps I suppose, but is a small part of the glue. To some we look alike. The biggest reason he's a best friend—he always makes me laugh; it's impossible for me to be in a bad mood when he's around or calls on the phone.

We both thrive on collecting anecdotes, reciting funny stories, quoting one-liners and creating self-parodies. Norman does it best. A recent example was his description of purchasing his first 'smartphone'. No techie, and with no knowledge except he wanted to get a "Droid", he found himself in a modern, glass-walled Phone Store at a local mall. An attractive young saleswoman, not reassured that he knew exactly what he wanted, or how to work any device he was considering, repeatedly asked him if she could provide instruction or help. Of course he declined, explaining that he knew exactly what he was doing. He proudly signed the credit card slip, pocketed his new phone, turned and, heading for the door, ran nose-first into a glass partition. And his problems continued, he reported. That night the phone kept waking him hourly saying "Droid, Droid" and he had no idea how to muffle it. And getting on a plane a few days later, when the preflight instruction to "turn off all electronic devices" was announced, he panicked, having no idea how to do that. I retell 'Norman stories' to people who don't even know him and get amused reactions.

Like all successful comedians, he also has a serious side, a thought provoking intellect and a reflective personality. We have as many serious discussions (politics, economics, medicine, family relationships, etc.) as laugh fests. I have few other friends about whom I could say the same. Furthermore, he has never disappointed me and has never offended me or made me angry. I may have no other friends like that.

It's always a mystery to me who, of all the people we encounter in life, turn out to be close friends. I have been lucky to find quite a few, and in that small group, Norman is one the best.

DEAR MARY LOU

Your son Ken Gleason Jr. called recently with the dreaded news; "Mother died yesterday, just three days past her 101st birthday. She was waiting for lunch with the visiting nurse in the living room when suddenly her breathing became irregular, then infrequent, and in minutes stopped."

My first thought was fierce regret at having not called or visited you in Newton in the recent several months. It's a bit late for my apologies now, so I'm sending this note—just for the record.

My next reflection has been 'how you'—how appropriate your final moments were peaceful and dignified. I also can't help wondering whether your signature, impish grin didn't flash one last time across your soft, round face.

Mary Louise Gleason, you and your husband Ken were New England originals. Kristin, I, and our 4 small children were immediately attracted to you both back in the 70's at Newton's Eliot Congregational Church. Our children needed surrogate grandparents nearby and you were a perfect fit. You knew, enjoyed and loved everyone in that congregation. Together and apart you radiated an aura of confident, calm welcoming. Moreover, you were the antithesis of our neighbors, many of whom were intense activists, ambitious intellectuals, and dedicated social butterflies.

Having successfully launched your children Ken Jr., Ellen and Connie, you blessed us by your willingness to be godparents to our 4 children Ian, Maria, Hannah and Jesse. Incidentally, you also became parental role-models for Kristin and me. All the visits, meals and holiday events we shared over 40 years are evidence that both families enjoyed and benefited from the happy arrangement.

I easily remember a plump, sturdy you greeting us at your front door with a cherubic smile, unruly white hair, bright eyes behind big glasses, doling out loving hugs with an endearing giggle. You always wanted to know everything about everyone else. You would eagerly talk about your adult children's lives, your 4 sisters and their lives, your friends and neighbors, but you rarely would mention yourself. And when you did, it was usually some silly mistake you had made, how badly you did things (like art), or how you wished you were a better person (something akin to the Dali Lama hoping for more serenity). Sorry, but I never bought your "I'm so hopeless" line.

You did leave one big mystery about yourself for me to ponder. How did you, among the most loving, forgiving and generous people ever, end up believing in late night conservative talk-radio and its dread-mongering, myth-spreading messages? Somehow, somewhere there may have been a fearful side of you that few of us knew about.

On a recent sunny, warm October Sunday afternoon they held your memorial service at Eliot Church. In that familiar, old sanctuary a big crowd of family and friends celebrated the great person they still hold dear.

Of course, the praise was effusive and the recollections laudatory. Knowing how self-effacing you always were, I kept thinking (to paraphrase from an eulogy about reticent E.B.White); "If Mary Lou could have been here today, she wouldn't have."

If I had been one of the speakers at that service, I would have added my own memories. I clearly recall how bemused you were to reach your 90's, and how bewildering 100 was. You faced serious health problems and some major surgery late in life with courage and perseverance. You took your dear husband Ken's death in stride and, although missing him terribly, never asked for sympathy or special treatment. Instead, you found joy and contentment in your family home on Garden Rd., especially the backyard porch and gardens you loved so much. Your conversation was always upbeat and hopeful, particularly when describing your own grandchildren.

Of course, I will always remember your sneaky sense of humor. I loved it when your poised granddaughter, 18 yo Ellie, related at the service that you told her that among the most important of your life's ingredients, the top ones were, in order, "chocolate, peanut butter and a husband."

Dear Mary Lou you lived long and well. If eternal bliss on the other side requires a person having been loving, modest, honest and thoroughly giving in this life, you qualify completely. Back here we are all hoping for your bliss, while we go on missing you thoroughly.

Sent with lots of love,

Ken

PS: Give Ian one of your great hugs for all of us, if possible.

ELLA WORKS THE PLAYGROUND

"HI. I'M ELLA," my 4 year old grand-daughter says to a group of young mothers watching their nearby toddlers at the Pond Park in Portsmouth. "I live at 44 Lawrence. This is my grandpa, Ken Fellows," she adds, gesturing toward me with a sweeping open hand like a television MC introducing a rock star. The mothers, many with baby bumps, flash bemused smiles.

Ella's parents are confirmed, middle-aged introverts. They are mortified by how gregarious she is. Even as extroverted as I am, her energetic engagement of the public is sometimes quite overwhelming. Then I consider that when you're 4, blond, blue-eyed and very cute, you can get away with a lot.

Perhaps because she's an only child, Ella seeks the attention and friendship of other children on the playground —and, she's usually successful at finding playmates quickly. She tends to use the direct approach; "Hi. I'm Ella. Want to be my friend today?" When turned down, she tells me "that one is shy" and moves on to another.

Ella recently told me; "I don't like boys. I only play with girls." When I reminded her that one of her favorite playmates, Brody, is a boy, she countered; "I do play with him. I pretend he's a girl."

She is not above making her frustrations with boys known to their caretakers. Some days ago, on a local playground she became irritated by a particularly loud and hyperactive boy of three. Identifying the boy's grandmother, Ella walked up to her and said; "Now, I'm a calm person, but he…" (I couldn't hear the rest). Of course, she isn't calm, but is hyperactive herself. In fact, she can get quickly out of control without adult supervision. But even such oversight can elicit an unexpected response, as the time I reprimanded her for overzealous play and she immediately turned to me, and with both hands on her chest, responded; "Grandpa, you hurt my heart."

Ella's surprising declarations aren't limited to encounters in the park. Riding in a car with Ella can be a hoot too, all the more entertaining because I'm driving and she's talking 'at' me from her car seat in the back. Recently while riding together she questioned whether I was really an adult. When I insisted I certainly was, she countered; "You're not an adult Grandpa, you don't even have a job." On another in-car occasion, I reminded her (yet again) that using the word 'please' was more effective than making a bold, unmodified demand. Her reply was; "OK. PLEASE hand me the book. But Grandpa, I won't be able to keep this up."

Impertinent, yes. But God, I love my loquacious grand-daughter.

ELLA GOODNIGHT

"Want to read another story, sweetheart?" I asked.

"No Grandpa, my eyes won't stay open," she whispered. "Let's just snuggle." A post-reading-cuddle is part of our bedtime ritual. It's my "BPOD" (Best Part Of the Day).

I had just hurried home from our Tuesday evening memoir writing class. There, a sleepy Kristin was well into a bedtime read with drowsy Ella, our five-year-old grand-daughter. Kristin eagerly slipped out of the bed as I entered the bedroom. Ella stared at me through half closed blue eyes. Her disheveled, long blonde hair gleaming in a shaft of light from a slit in a tattered bedside lampshade.

I tug the tarnished, beaded chain that douses the bedside light. The room quiets except for the faint roar of the furnace on this cold winter night. A 'Christmas electric candle' in the bedroom window glows faintly behind a drawn shade, providing dim but warm, yellow light. Ella's shoulders are covered by her "nigh-night," a thin, greyish-blue infant cover which offers her loyal security with its homey smell and fuzzy feel. The rest of her is hidden under a heavy white comforter.

I lie down beside her. Eyes closed, she squirms toward me until her forehead nestles under my chin. Ten little fingers gently enfold my right hand and pull it to her chest. Within seconds her body stills. Her breathing slows. Her hands twitch every few seconds, but maintain their tender grip. In a minute, all her muscles relax. She's sound asleep.

Ella's soft, clean hair and smooth forehead are right there next to my lips. I don't have to move an inch to kiss her. Her head smells as delightful as when she was a newborn.

Gazing downward I can see only her closed left eye and adjacent round cheek, both enlarged because she's so close. They're so sculptural I want to sketch them... right then. Squinting further down between us, I make-out a jumble of scruffy teddy bears and other stuffed animals. Her favorite, grey-brown "Mr. Rabbit" sits atop the heap. He's much bigger than the others and possesses some of Ella's own distinctive features; long, disjointed legs and floppy arms loosely attached to a slim, sturdy torso. Mr. Rabbit and her nigh-night are rarely out of her reach all night long.

Ella's bed is a family heirloom, rickety and squeaky despite heavy head and foot boards supported by turned mahogany bed-posts. It's the only bed my paternal grandparents ever owned and likely where my father was conceived. Ella is the 5th generational occupant.

We snuggle about fifteen minutes before heavy drowsiness overcomes me. The world around us so still and calm, I struggled to leave. I wonder; would I like to go on lying here forever, or would I rather just die because nothing else could ever be as peaceful?

Post Script:

Some might ask, didn't you have the same or similar

moments with your own children? I enjoyed bedtime reading with them immensely and did it often. But I was busier then, and more intense. I was usually reading to 3 or 4 at once, rarely only one.

Also, I had weighty distractions—a growing family, a developing career, an uncertain academic future. There wasn't the same space then...the dedicated free time...the years of acquired perspective.

I loved my own children, and being with them, as much as being with Ella. It's my bliss that's greater now, not my love.

AN INTERNATIONAL ADOPTION

THE 1X2, B&W PHOTO presented a scrawny, six-month-old Korean baby with spikey, black hair above a grim, thin face. His name: Kim Hak Soo. His history: "male infant left in a basket on doorstep of Korean Police Station." And so it began.

He was the baby "match" Holt International Adoptions offered Kristin and me in 1972. He was to be our 3rd child, following our 'birthed children' Ian (4) and Hannah (2). Can you bond with a child's picture? Can you love a child before you even meet him? It turns out you can. Jesse Kim (his new name) needed a family; we wanted him. That's all it takes.

Our decision to adopt had been decided years before. Kristin and I were driving a highway one day early in our marriage, discussing how many children we might have. Without much debate the answer just evolved, like the consensus at a Quaker Meeting. We would have 4 children; 2 naturally, 2 adopted. Jesse moved the plan ahead another step. It was completed a couple of years later when we adopted Maria Camacho (8) from Columbia.

Jesse was flown to us in Boston accompanied by a

Holt Adoption Service attendant. Clean and healthy, he was as skinny as his pictures, but smiley. When upset, his cry was high pitched and riveting. Arriving in summer, he perspired profusely. He didn't smell like an American baby; for months his odor was pungent and spicy, as if he had been dipped in kimchi. He was 'especially adopted' by his two-year-old sister, Hannah, who eagerly informed friends and passersby inspecting her new little brother; "He named Korea." After fattening on American baby food, he became plump and cute. He slimmed way down as a child and an adult, becoming thin, muscular and uncommonly handsome.

Jesse grew up to be a loving, sociable, intelligent young man. But not without difficulty. Dyslexia turns out to be very common among adopted Korean boys. His was moderately so, and required two high school years of special education, a severe embarrassment in his adolescence. It also contributed to his failing college his first semester there.

All the schools he attended were predominantly white (or "pink" as my friend Paul says). All of his friends were white too, but they generally considered him the 'leader of the pack.' Quiet and stoic, he offered little about his inner feelings to us and never mentioned any inhibitions about his dark skin and Asian face. Once, in 1st grade, he said a boy threw a punch and a racial slur his way.

"How did you feel? What did you do?" I asked.

"I kicked him in the balls," was his stone-faced response.

In his 20's, Jesse graduated culinary school to become a chef in San Francisco, Ann Arbor, and Philadelphia over fifteen years. He then went back to college to obtain a degree in Food Science. For the past several years he has successfully headed a food laboratory for the Campbell Soup Co. A seven year marriage ended in divorce some years ago, but his girlfriend Erin has been a constant in his life since.

Recently, I sent him a *New York Times* article; "The Returned." It described a number of Korean adoptees in the US, now adults in their 30's and 40's, who feel they were inappropriately deprived of their natural Korean heritage, customs, language, and culture, and have moved back to Seoul to regain what they missed. They also seek to promote changes in Korean law and customs to make it harder in the future to adopt from that country. Although many of those returnees are highly resentful of having been brought up in an alienating white society, others are just ambivalent about their parents, families and life in N. America. Because Jesse never expressed interest in his Korean origins or in even visiting Korea, I didn't expect much reaction to the piece, or even a reply. I received both.

He wrote this to me; "…I found myself fighting back tears many times…I can relate to about 99% of the article."

"It wasn't until I was about 16 that I felt comfortable seeing myself in the mirror…I was in shock that I was different and that I hadn't suddenly become white. I avoided making eye contact with my reflection in any mirror."

"I've never had an Asian girlfriend, not for a lack of attraction but maybe for the same sociological reason… believing I am white."

"I will always be grateful for the opportunities that my loving parents provided me and I never discount that…I am proud to be part of your legacies. I also believe I am your son and that many of my beliefs and ethics have been passed from you to me…I love you both and will always appreciate the life you have provided."

Jesse's detailed reactions surprised, saddened,

and inspired Kristin and me. We sent them on to his sisters who also admitted being tearful and shocked at the depth of his long suppressed emotions suddenly revealed.

So, it turns out, international adoption is more complicated, more nuanced, more layered than we imagined. Some of its joys and problems are well-known, while others are still being discovered. Like the mother who wrote the *Times'* article, I hope I can answer my adult-children's questions "without defensiveness — and with candor and empathy. I need to remember (that) two things may be true simultaneously: Our (children) love us — and need to question how we became a family."

PRODIGAL CHILD

I was there Dec. 27, 1972, at Boston's Lying in Hospital, the moment my daughter Hannah was born . She entered this world annoyed—a dark haired, wailing baby—protesting her fate.

The second of our four children, her birth was the only one I attended (not invited to Ian's birth; Jesse and Maria were adopted). Despite her demonstrative beginning, Hannah became one of the cutest, most agreeable toddlers imaginable—a pigtailed, exuberant charmer who most evenings delighted me with a boisterous welcome-home "Daadie," shouted as if I had been gone for months.

From early age, she was a natural caretaker for her two adopted siblings. Jesse was the first under her wing. "Imported" by us, he was seven-month-old Kim Hak Soo, whom Hannah (age three) introduced to others as "He named Korea." When Hannah was six she became the guardian-sister for Maria, who at eight arrived from Columbia speaking only Spanish. As Maria's first protector and guide, language proved no barrier. Their sister-ship was immediate and endured until Maria went off to Smith College. However stressed their adult relationship has been from interval events, they have remained concerned cross-country sisters, Hannah in New England, Maria in the Southwest.

Grade-school, middle and high school were not easy for Hannah. She was increasingly introspective and obsessed by what friends and classmates thought of her. She and next-door best friend Amy perched for hours after school in a gigantic Copper Beach tree across from our Farlow Rd. home in Newton, discussing LIFE. Shifting alliances among girlfriends were a frequent concern. Her studies and school activities were not compelling. She was a very good soccer player, and so was Maria. Distaining the competition and comparison, Hannah abruptly retired from soccer and all sports at the beginning of Middle School.

Despite her inquisitive mind, a mimicking sense of humor, and obvious intelligence, academically Hannah was loyal to the grade of C. This caused some frustration for her parents who knew she had more potential. Hannah's proudest moment in high school may have been her graduation day. Not only did she get a diploma, but she (later) revealed that she was nude under her cap and gown. That daring accomplishment reflected another of her characteristics — a penchant for risk taking.

Hannah's college career, in search of an art degree, started at the Savannah School of Art and Design. After 2 years, she migrated to the San Francisco Art Institute, finding herself in that city along with siblings Jesse and Maria — not entirely by coincidence. Our children knew California from several childhood trips to visit Kristin's parents in Laguna Beach. They all decided back then that, when someday independent, they intended to move to the West Coast. So they all did, at just about the same time.

San Francisco presented Hannah with a new list of distractions and indulgences: a long-term boyfriend who was calm but flawed, some friends exploring a fast life, and a hostess' job at the Top of the Mark which provided access to a walk on the wild side. As her life's direction wobbled, she progressively distanced herself from siblings and parents.

Leaving the boyfriend and San Francisco after a few years, she returned to Philadelphia to make her way as a radio advertising executive, a job she loved, but it ended in an economic downturn. In her 30's and living with an old boyfriend from high school, she was in the same city as her parents and older brother Ian, but socially withdrawn. Interchanges happened, but were infrequent and stressing. Information about her life was vague and inconsistent. Loving her as much as ever, she seemed lost to us. And lost to herself. We moved to Kittery in retirement; she stayed in Philadelphia.

And then a turnaround—begun with the boyfriend going to prison for drug dealing. Fed up with her lifestyle, Hannah initiated a personal recovery in Philly. When that was only partly successful, Hannah returned home to Kittery and some parental support. Over 2-3 rocky years she had a series of service jobs, devoted a month to an inpatient recovery program and briefly attended a local hair-styling school. Eventually, she moved to a Portsmouth apartment as her mind cleared and she reestablished purpose in her life. A happy job at the Press Room in Portsmouth eventually led to meeting and marrying Mike Marchand—and then to the birth of Ella Elizabeth Marchand, May 28, 2008.

Ella's arrival was a blessing for the whole family. The grief attendant to Ian's sudden death in 2006 was still present, but considerably dissipated by the new baby. Hannah had prophesied at Ian's funeral that his death would bring our family "closer together," which happened and was then reinforced by Ella's birth.

With the joys and responsibilities of motherhood,

Hannah found restored confidence and a regained equilibrium. From the start, she has been a great mother—way better than the acceptable 'good enough.' She and Ella are devoted to each other, occasional, brief conflicts notwithstanding. As Hannah and Mike's marriage foundered, the mother-daughter bond strengthened. An inevitable divorce, when Ella was five, happened quickly and with minimum drama. Afterward, their family dynamics actually seem improved: Mike lives in Portsmouth, sees Ella at least weekly and helps in her parenting.

Newly motivated, Hannah waitressed while also studying for enough college credits to quality for nursing school at Great Bay Community College. She attained her RN degree *with honors* in 2015! She surprised herself and gratified her parents with such academic success. She and brother Jesse, former college drop-outs, found the resourcefulness and motivation not only to eventually graduate, but to achieve their degrees with honors, turnabouts bordering on the miraculous. Hannah began her nursing career locally in 2016. She has the confidence, knowledge and mentality to be a compassionate, successful caregiver.

Dear Hannah once was lost, but now is found. Amazing grace.

MEMORIES

GROWING UP I

MY YOUNG DOCTOR-FATHER AND NURSE-MOTHER married after meeting at Blodgett Hospital in Grand Rapids (MI). I was born at Blodgett in 1938, the first of four (three boys, one girl). We lived in a tree-shaded, three bedroom, two story, red brick house much like the other small, tree-shaded brick and stucco houses nestled along one side of Alexander St.. Across the street was a big public park, center stage for my childhood.

Franklin Park was a large square, two blocks on each side. It contained open grassy plots between clumps of tall trees and several teeter-tottered, jungle-gymed play areas. Also, a dozen tennis courts and two ball diamonds. In winter the softball field was flooded for skating, while a nearby wide, steep hill provided great sledding.

In the park's center was a large, wooden pavilion accommodating three basketball courts where rough, African-American kids rudely introduced me to the basics of basketball. An ungifted player, it wasn't until college that I became even mediocre, but I kept at it as an adult into retirement, playing pick-up B-ball weekly into my late 70's. Attached to the pavilion was an outdoor, eight-lane swimming pool, the incubator of my competitive high school and college swimming. Summer for me was determined not by the calendar or weather, but by the day the city filled the Franklin Park pool.

Warm, humid mid-western summer days I often awoke to eerie, staccato cooing sounds, which I curiously imagined were noises made by nuns who occasionally walked by our house in their spooky habits. At six years I knew nothing about bird-calls and had never heard of morning doves. On some of those mornings I waited curbside for the milkman's arrival. It was the mid-1940's and milk was delivered from green and yellow painted, enclosed, spoke-wheeled, horse-drawn wagons. For me, the horse was a big attraction. They were solitary, thin animals of calm demeanor, plodding pace and the ability to stop without command in front of each subscribers' house. The milk was kept in wooden cases behind the driver, cooled there by great hunks of block ice. The fragrance of those wagons was distinctive—a sweet mixture of milky ice-melt, wet wagon wood and horsehair smells. The biggest thrill those early mornings was persuading the milkman to let me ride on the wagon a few stops, sometimes getting to feed the horse a carrot at the end.

Most summer mornings I was off to the park by 9 am for the opening of the pool. I was there so much in summertime, and so familiar with the lifeguards, I imagined myself part of the staff, or at least their mascot. I tried my extroverted best to be persistently helpful, loquacious and clownish. After several years (I was about nine then), I greeted the senior adult lifeguard one opening day saying; "Hi Doug, I'm Kenny. Don't you remember me?" He replied; "Remember you? Of course I do. You haunt me!"

Spending the better part of every summer day at the

Franklin Park pool, I learned how to swim well, quickly. My first year I won a qualifying free-style race for pre-K kids, sending me to that summer's All City Swim Meet. I could swim fast for a 6 year old, but lacked any real racing skills. Confident that I could out swim the others in my race, I actually just jumped off the starting block (I'd never tried a racing dive), and proceeded to weave my way down the roped racing lane, bouncing off the marker buoys, 50 yards to a crushing 2nd place finish. In front of a crowd that included my mother and siblings, I was shocked and embarrassed. In fact, the defeat I absorbed turned out to be appropriate preparation for my aquatic future. I went on to have a dedicated, but ultimately modest, swimming career in high school and college (even after developing a competent racing dive and improved navigational sense). Unfortunately, I never mastered a competitive 'flip-turn', which resulted in my accumulating a whole box full of mostly pink 3rd and purple 4th place ribbons.

Ice hockey was the game I had the most fun playing, so learning to skate at age 5 or 6 on the flooded park softball diamond has been an indelible memory. The task was not easy for a chubby boy not strong or flexible enough to properly lace his own skates.

To go skating there was a ritual: first, I bundled up at home in musty layers of sweater, puffy jacket, and baggy leggings; after getting scratchy stocking feet into stiff hockey skates, a parent tightened the laces with a button-hook, no less. I then trudged off (with my skates on) through deep snow to the rink 10 minutes away. I was pretty exhausted by the time I got there.

The park's skating rink also facilitated a sexual awakening in early adolescence. Maybe it was the bright moon and starry skies accentuating their rosy cheeks and noses, but even stocking hatted and thickly scarfed, the opposite sex was intriguing. A defining moment occurred one winter evening when 2 pretty, agile skating girls we had been noticing approached my friend and me. With utter self-confidence, they flipped each of us a coin, one of them calling over her shoulder; "Here's a nickel, phone us in a couple of years." What a shock. Who knew…mutual attraction?

It turns out the pleasure of skating has been enduring. Late in life I'm still playing some pond hockey and teaching my grand-daughter Ella to skate — pure pleasure too.

GROWING UP II

WE PLAYED SANDLOT BASEBALL on vacant fields and in backyards. The Franklin Park baseball diamond was reserved for high school and college play, and the softball field was used afternoons and evenings for industrial league and semi-pro games. Being in the park most of every summer, I managed to insert myself into those league games as a self- appointed batboy and retriever of foul balls. As with the lifeguards at the pool, I ingratiated myself to a seasonally recurring group of teenagers and adults by being perpetually self-promoting, pretentious and mouthy. Looking back, my shamelessness is cringe-worthy, if not worse.

In autumn, I spent endless hours playing 'pass and tap' (no tackling) football on cool, crisp late afternoons, the air smelling of bonfires burning around the neighborhood.

Home from school around 3:30, I changed clothes on the fly, gulped down a Coke and peanut butter sandwich, then headed off to the park with a gang of boys and a football. We played until hunger, dark or an exasperated father (usually mine) intervened.

My hero in those games was 'Chuck Ortman', then the

star quarterback of the U. of Michigan football team. A color photo of him hung on my bedroom wall. Playing, I mimicked his moves and mannerisms as I saw in them in occasional movies of Michigan games (no TV then). I tried to be his replica, religiously wearing a "49" on my maize 'n blue Michigan football jersey. I kept both sleeves rolled up above my elbows, "just like Chuck" I would explain to friends.

Hero worshipping recurred fifteen years later, when I was a 3rd year medical student in Ann Arbor, just beginning my clinical years. There Dr. Richard Judge, a thin, intense, soft-spoken young cardiologist, became in a few minutes of medical drama, the model physician I aspired to be.

One hot, late hospital afternoon, Dr. Judge was leading our eager group of 8 medical students from bed to bed down a long medical ward, stopping to discuss each patient's case history and pertinent physical findings. Quite suddenly a middle-aged man near us fell from his bed in cardiac arrest. Dr. Judge calmly and gracefully jumped over the bed to straddle the man's torso. Almost in the same motion he administered a one handed, heart rattling 'thump' to the patient's sternum. Regaining his feet and composure and without raising his voice or showing any indecision, he then orchestrated a tense, forty-five-minute resuscitation involving a cast of excited but efficient additional doctors and nurses. The man survived. After all that drama I saw no change in Dr. Judge's appearance or demeanor. He resumed rounds as if nothing had happened.

In my subsequent forty-year career in academic medicine, he was my model. I even sub-specialized in (pediatric) cardiology. I compulsively had white coats tailored to reach just the mid-thigh level, and favored blue shirts with bow-ties, because that was his style. My professional affect was friendly and informed, composed and controlled. In emergencies, as medical colleagues raised the level of excitement, stress and action, the calmer I became and the slower I moved, still maintaining maximum intention and purpose. I made myself into a Dr. Richard Judge clone of sorts. When I retired he was still alive and practicing in Ann Arbor, so I wrote him a letter to tell him how influential he had been for me, and to thank him for his inspirational demeanor.

GROWING UP III

My mother, Bernice ("Mom"), was a strong, steady and loving fixture for me. Because her parents died in her childhood, she was raised in a small, Michigan town (Greenville, near Grand Rapids) by her Uncle Bob Cornelius and wife Marie. Independent and smart, she became a surgical scrub nurse at Blodgett hospital in GR. She recalled that when she first met her future husband there she found him "arrogant." My father always used that reference to point out "the fine line between love and hate." My father was smart too, both practical and 'street-smart." Neither was an intellectual; mother's reading was mostly The Reader's Digest (a periodically published distillation of contemporary books), while my Dad read medical books and journals almost exclusively, his only diversion being the magazine 'Popular Mechanics'. Both were staunch Midwestern Republicans, an embarrassment to me from adolescence on. My stoic mother's biggest asset was her capacity for 'acceptance'; when things went badly she could always soldier on; "oh well, nothing you can do about it" was her common reaction. I missed getting that maternal gene.

My father once apologized while driving our car

with 14yo me beside him. [Cars are good place to have a frank discussion because both driver and passenger are fixed on the road ahead; the absence of eye contact makes intimacy somehow easier] He said he regretted spending most of his life working and not devoting more time to family play and vacations. I told him I had no regrets and his apology was unnecessary. I have many fond memories of the time he spent with me and my siblings. We fished together, we played catch endlessly, we had a well used Ping-Pong table (and then a pool-table) in our basement, he built a small sailboat for us, we played tennis and waterskied throughout my youth, and we took a number of family vacations in Michigan when we weren't having fun at our summer cottage on Whitefish Lake, close to Grand Rapids. In fact I had a happy childhood.

My father was a disciplinarian, and I was expected to work too (yardman at home and the cottage, house painting, pet care, babysitting, etc.). He also expected my best effort on every job. He placed a premium on the work ethic in our family life, too much so for my mother's taste. His emphasis on always taking all the time needed to do a job well, and never being reluctant to work harder or longer than the other guy, were lessons that served me well, and ones I tried do pass on to my children.

If any of my athleticism was inherited, it was my father who was the source. My dear mother was an ardent sports fan, but by her own assessment, no athlete. In high school she participated in no sports, but liked being a spectator to most. She was the statistician over several years for the (boys') varsity basketball team. As an adult she maintained her enthusiasm for collegiate and professional sports. There was a baseball, football or hockey broadcast going in our house most of the time. When I didn't understand the rules or the action,

Mom could usually explain. Sports were just a part of our life, conversation and interest.

My father was a sports fan too, but less knowledgeable than my mother. He was athletic too, despite my grandparents pushing him to be a professional musician and to earn money working when he wasn't practicing the violin. Somehow, he managed to be an 18-year-old city tennis champion the same year he was playing violin in the Grand Rapids Symphony. He grew up across the street from a (different) city park where he was taught tennis by his father, as my father later taught me in Franklin Park.

Playing baseball catch in the backyard or in the street was the "sport" Dad and I spent the most time doing together. We were often joined by my brother John, rarely by brother Rick or sister Marcia, and never by Mom (she didn't DO sports). My father pitched some while in the Army during WWII: we worked on who could throw the best curveball and other techniques, but mostly just for relaxation time after dinner.

As a kid and preadolescent, my father often took me cold autumn evenings to the Ottawa Hills High School games, the high school I eventually attended. He had gone to South High School (also in Grand Rapids), incidentally at the same time President Gerald Ford did. In early adolescence, I was elated to begin driving with him, Mom and sometimes another couple to Ann Arbor, a three-hour one-way trip back then, to attend Saturday afternoon Michigan football games. Although only one or two times each fall, those exciting journeys were highlights in my youth, some of my best memories. And it wasn't just the spectacle — the mighty maize and blue helmeted team, one of the world's best marching bands, the famous Hail to the Victors fight song repeatedly sung with gusto by 100,000 or more delirious fans. There also was our traditional stop for dinner at *Win Schuler's*, one of Michigan's most popular restaurants, at the midway point of the postgame, homeward drive. The wait for a table in that sprawling eatery was often an hour or more, but the expensive meals were especially delicious and the atmosphere electric, since all the patrons were still revved up from that day's football game in either Ann Arbor or East Lansing (home of Michigan State).

If I had to pick a favorite day, or time, from my childhood it would be very difficult. I was fortunate enough to have had mostly good times and happy days. Forced to choose, I'd probably go with a family trip to Ann Arbor to see a football game. Followed by a game of catch if we got home in time.

MOVIES AT HOME

BACK IN THE 1950s, before television there were home shown movies. Some were 'home movies', those clichéd documentaries of mundane family life and tedious summer vacations. Far better were the professional films rented from the local drugstore—early (B&W) Mickey and Minnie Mouse cartoons, and short features starring the Little Rascals and ("Soytenly, Soytenly") the Three Stooges.

On occasional snowy winter nights Dad drove downtown to select 3 or 4 films, taking me along as 'film critic'. By the time we were back the buttery smell of popcorn permeated the house. My mother and 3 bathrobed siblings were sprawled on the living room couch excited and anxious for the show to begin.

We owned a finicky projector which my father ran until I took over as a preteen. That little 8mm film projector, with its sewing machine sized motor, emitted two distinct smells. The first was a pungently metallic, oily aroma from the spinning drive-sprockets. Flipping on the bright projector bulb caused a separate smell —hot and acrid. Those evocative smells joined the clickety-click sound of the thimble shaped sprockets that propelled the celluloid film from the high, front 'feeding' reel to the low, back 'take-up reel.'

The movies were projected on a wobbly 3x4' silvered screen. We kids sat shoulder to shoulder on the couch or floor, popcorn spilling down flannel pajamas, our anticipation rising as the large numbers on the screen counted down... 4...3...2...1, leading soundlessly to... THE TITLE. After a few short credits, the sudden appearance of Mickey, Spanky, or Larry, Moe and Curly in our own living room was magical. Everything on the screen was funnier, sadder and more intense than it ever was in a theater, or later on TV. The movies were soundless, but the small audience was loud and animated: laughter, shrieks, and roll around, leg kicking excitement prevailed.

The sprockets spun and clicked, the film jumped and wiggled through movie after movie, each one concluding with "THE END", followed by a familiar flap...flap...flap as the film's free-end circled the take-up reel.

Those movies at home are something I miss from my childhood. My 4 year old grand-daughter Ella is thoroughly disbelieving when I tell her we didn't have television, computers, or iPads. She has always had, at hand, almost any cartoon or kid's movie ever made...in stunning color with surround sound on a 60" HD screen in the living room or on a lap-top monitor in her bed.

I often wonder if that's better. No doubt what she watches is generally more educational and artistic. I worry that she often watches alone or with someone else in the room who is doing something else. Like much contemporary television viewing or computer browsing, it's not a time for togetherness. It seems we have to wait every few years for the televised Olympic Games to have something whole families gather around to share.

Ella also will have no machinery smells or distinctive sounds to remind her of the first cartoons she watched —a loss she won't know since she can't miss what she never experienced. Perhaps I should get her an app, so that when she turns on the computer, popcorn smells and hot bulb aromas blow through the room, and the end of each cartoon is accompanied by THE END... flap...flap...flap.

MY LIFE IN MUSIC

MY DREADED PIANO LESSONS BEGAN at age 8. At my parents' insistence I practiced almost daily on an ebony baby-grand Steinway that dominated our tiny living room. I persevered 4 or 5 difficult, frustrating and tormented years before they abandoned their musical hopes for me. My failure also discouraged my folks from any musical ambitions for my 3 trailing siblings. Even though my father played violin as a teen well enough to be the Grand Rapids city orchestra, and my mother played piano, they accepted their children's non-musicality graciously.

Talent, motivation, inspiration —I lacked all the necessary prerequisites for making music. The whole experience left me justifiably humbled. Many other endeavors came to me with some ease; sports, studying, social interactions.

Piano was my boyhood Waterloo.

Lacking playing ability was inhibiting enough, but I was also stressed by the site of the lessons. Biweekly I was driven downtown to a grey stone Convent whose steep steps led to tall, imposing, Saint-engraved wooden doors. Just climbing those stairs to announce my arrival through a door-side speaker sent my heart racing. Sister Elizabeth, my piano teacher, was a thin faced nun, austere but kind, who usually held a small crucifix in her porcelain white hands while letting me in. On entering the bare, high ceilinged foyer, I faced a large, wall-mounted sculpture of Jesus on the Cross. I didn't know the phrase then, but thinking back I 'really felt His pain' every time I entered there. Sister would lead me to a sunbaked, antique smelling room just off the foyer where waited a weathered, old upright piano, the instrument of my impending torture. There for 45 minutes I stuttered and stumbled by way over the keyboard with Sister sitting next to me, until both of us were exhausted. I truly hope someone, sometime, recommended that nun for sainthood; her patience in the face of my ineptitude was inspirational, maybe divine.

Sister E. wasn't the only teacher to suffer my incompetence. Mr. Mitchell, the twitchy but patient Music Director for Ottawa Hills High School, auditioned me as a pianist but immediately diverted me to the percussion section of the Marching Band and the Senior Orchestra. This solved two problems for him; my piano playing would not be a musical distraction, and he needed bodies to play the drums, cymbals and other simple instruments. I discovered I had a pretty good sense of rhythm. I loved traveling with the band to football games and participating with the orchestra in state-wide competitions. Among my recollections are two special ones as a percussionist:

On one cold fall night as a H.S senior, for the finale each instrumental section of the marching band performed a solo piece and then ran off the field. The drum section was the last remaining group, and following our solo, all but I (the bass drummer), ran to the sidelines. As scripted, I looked around confused and surprised, improvised my own rhythmic solo, doffed my band hat, bowed low, and ran off too. Imagine! Me the "featured musician.

Another memorable event arose from a state wide, high school orchestral competition. I fretted about whether, as the tympanist who must endure many measures of nothing to do, I could come in on time and in tune (tympanies must be tuned on the fly). After the competition our orchestra was listening to a recording of the performance and a critique by Mr. Mitchell. At some point in his commentary, he blurted, "Tympanies in tune." No other praise in my life has ever been as sweet.

Two minor triumphs in several years of musical practice, embarrassment and failure are not much to hang on to, but they are what I have. I was fortunate in marrying a wife who was naturally musical and brought joy to our family with her singing and guitar playing (and she looked like Joan Baez). She even had the patience to let me join family song fests playing the auto-harp, but only on the condition that I not sing. Anyway, the reduced and clearly annotated keyboard of the auto-harp was perfect for me.

Fortunately, my profound deficiencies in making music never diminished my enjoyment of music. Even in my dotage, music of all sorts… classical, folk, instrumental, solo voice, group and choral… is a part of my life whether working around the house, painting in my studio, or just relaxing. I can't imagine life without it.

AUDITORIUM DREAD

THE FOUR AISLED, SLOPING FLOOR of the Ottawa Hills High School Auditorium supported 400 creaky, wooden seats facing a wide, dark green curtained stage. That single venue was the site of several indelible, coming-of-age events in my life.

JR. HIGH ORCHESTRA

In the 8th grade I was a reluctant member of the Ottawa Junior High Orchestra. My deficient musical talent had been exposed in rehearsals, resulting in my 'promotion' to Announcer for the Annual Spring Concert. Free'd from the pressures of inept musicianship, I then stressed over becoming a public speaker. I was a childhood stutterer whose habit was only partially controlled after several years of speech therapy.

Stuttering was a problem I couldn't fix with practice. There were always particular words lying-in-wait, however much I rehearsed, to instill fear and threaten embarrassment. Talking slowly helped, but didn't prevent the humiliating, repetitive grinding on the first syllable of certain words that were my nemesis. I aimed to do the best I could, knowing that my mother would be there: I didn't want to embarrass her too.

Facing hundreds of students and adults in the High School Auditorium, I did better than expected, but not as well as I hoped. I stumbled and stuttered a bit through a long list of compositions, composers and solo artists. My ever-supportive mother told me I did well, as did many others. Nonetheless, the tension, anxiety and chagrin of that experience is ever linked to that place.

ATHLETIC AWARDS NIGHT

In an undistinguished 4-year high school athletic career, through shear perseverance, I managed to 'letter' in baseball and swimming. On a swim-team of about 15 boys, I was the 5th or 6th fastest. My baseball playing was enthusiastic, but relegated to reserve roles. In my senior year I was appointed 3rd base coach: my baseball skills were spotty, but I understood the game and could holler volumes of baseball trash talk.

The only time I ever excelled athletically was in a strength and endurance competition between the school's jocks. I managed 157 consecutive crunches, a school record which lasted about an hour until Tony Bott, a star football player, outdid me by doing 160. Feeling the agony of defeat, I reluctantly attended the Varsity Letter Club's award ceremony in the auditorium that year without ever mentioning the event to my parents.

SENIOR CLASS PLAY

In the 12th grade I had a minor part in the play "Cheaper by the Dozen." The first evening's performance in the Ottawa auditorium was attended by my mother but not my father, who stayed at home with a baby (late marriage surprise) brother.

A scene mid-play called for a teen couple, alone on stage, to attempt a first kiss. Type-casted as the girl's annoying brother, I was to stroll on stage munching a peanut butter sandwich, and as the kiss was about to happen, to utter; "Aha, caught you guys." Timed right, it was an easy laugh.

Opening night, it didn't go smoothly. I hated mayonnaise...never ate it...never knew anyone combined it with peanut butter. As I entered stage-right I unwittingly took a big chomp of the bread hiding that diabolical combination. I immediately gagged and choked my line, trying hard not to retch. The audience loved it, thinking it was part of the act. My mother said she hadn't detected my gasping discomfort. I checked the sandwich ingredients carefully before each of the subsequent performances.

GRADUATION AWARDS NIGHT

One week before graduation I was in the auditorium for the last time. I and about 20 other seniors were seated on the stage, having been informed of certain awards and scholarships to be presented. The audience was the entire student body, our teachers and a scattering of parents, mine among them. Both parents! That unprecedented occurrence seemed strange since I was in line for only a minor prize: 'Junior Rotarian of 1956.' I thought my father's rare presence was because he was a Rotarian.

The top awards were reserved for the end of the program. First, the prestigious 'Daughters of the American Revolution' award was given to the senior female showing the highest scholastic, participatory and athletic achievement. It went to my high school girlfriend, Jane Morley. She deserved it and I was excited for her.

I sat there engrossed in thoughts about Jane's success. I barely noticed that our H.S. Principal, Elmo Werringa, had moved on to his description of the 'William S. Upton Award' for the all-around-male in the class. Several candidates flashed casually through my mind: Walt Jolly was smart and affable, Mike Coddington a great athlete, and John Cowlishaw a brilliant student. Hard choice.

As the Principal concluded his remarks saying, "The Upton award goes to the male who consistently dots his i's and crosses his t's," I was still in a distracted, Jane-centered trance. I vaguely heard him say "and this year's honor goes to…!"

What? Me?? 'Must be a mistake…maybe a joke? Then it dawned on me: it could be true… 'probably the reason my parents were *both* there for the first time ever that I could remember. My next thought was…finally something had gone right in that old auditorium.

CHRISTMAS PRESENT

AT AGE 10, IT OCCURRED TO ME that Christmas giving, while unlikely to be better that receiving, might be something I should try doing. For my mother. A big stimulus for this unprecedented thoughtfulness was the rumor that a big, downtown department store in Grand Rapids, 'Herpolsheimers,' was offering a gift orchid with any purchase. What could be more exotic for a naïve Midwestern kid than a colorful orchid from the jungles of wherever? I had to get one. And I was not without resources. Work was strongly encouraged (especially lawn mowing) in our family, and it was well compensated.

We lived only a 15 minute bus ride from the downtown stores. Several pals and I decided to shop in secret for our mothers' presents. Since it was the first time on public transportation without a parent for each of us, it was a BIG ADVENTURE.

Getting on the bus was easy: it was only a block from my house. Knowing where and how to get off the bus was the problem. Fortunately, Herpolsheimers' Department Store was near the medical office building where my father worked, and I recognized the area when we got close. It's likely some adults helped too. Because we had no real problems getting downtown and back, I recall an immense sense of accomplishment and a huge expansion of my world, way beyond where my legs and bike had taken me before.

The store itself was 50's modern —its "soaring" (3-4 story) glassed front and electric doors memorable, and the vastness of each level bewildering. And I was no neophyte. My mother had dragged me through Marshall Field's famous store on past trips to Chicago. It was those trips that instilled in me a general aversion to shopping that has been life-long.

I eventually found a present where utility and my $10 limit converged; a stylish, chrome-metal device for women to attach to the edge of a restaurant table from which to hang their purse. Perfect! What mother wouldn't want one? I recall the meager sale price didn't qualify me for a coveted free orchid, but the saleswoman was so smitten by my mission that she gave me the flower anyway. It was anticlimactic. The bloom was small, mostly white and half wilted, struggling to survive in a water-filled glass tube with an afixed lapel-pin for attaching to a dress or coat.

My mother, as always, was gracious and grateful in accepting the purse-hanger, and "delighted" by the nearly dead orchid. The occasion was a milestone for me: I had become at once, adventurous, generous and worldly.

TIGHT SPOTS

It started as fun on a sweltering Michigan summer afternoon in the mid-1950's. Tommy McConnel's black Model T Ford coupe was chugging up a narrow gravel road that peaked high above Sand Lake before its steep, curving descent to the lake's swimming beach. Clinging to that rusty antique, we were a carefree, "immortal" teenage gang—Tommy driving, 2 more kids crowded in the cab, 2 on each running-board, 2 balancing on the back bumper, and Bonnie and I in the rumble seat—just cruising the back country roads of Western Michigan.

The Model T recently had been completely dismantled and then reassembled by 17-year-old Tommy—with only 4 or 5 machine parts left over. It was amazing to us; 5 perfectly good, but completely nonessential, components! [I've since heard that if one takes apart and puts back together an old car three times, there will be enough parts in the end for two cars]

We were a group of 10-12 friends whose families for years summered in adjacent cottages Big Whitefish Lake. Equally boys and girls, we were together much of the time in July and August swimming and diving from a communal raft, fishing, camping out, racing small outboard motor boats and lip-synching rock n' roll songs in weekly garage parties. Bonnie and I were the only "couple" — we were having a 'first kiss' romance that summer — a big frustration for my rival in this affair who, incidentally, was driving the car. Perhaps our being together in the rumble seat was a distraction for him.

As the over-loaded coupe reached the summit above Sand Lake, an on-coming car emerged in our path. Tommy veered to the right, crashing into something with a crunching thud, our sudden stop enveloped by dense, choking dust. After the air cleared, we were all still aboard and unhurt, but the front wheels and half of the hooded motor were hanging over a precipice about 100 feet above the lake. A flimsy wooden guardrail and a pile of dirt behind it had prevented a long plunge into the blue water below. Shaken, but maintaining our adolescent bravado, we staggered out to survey the scene.

Someone ran off to call a wrecker and our parents. Waiting there, our swagger waned as it dawned on us how fortunate we had been. Probably no more group Model-T soirees for us.

At some time most awaken to the possibility of their own mortality. That was my moment. Also, as it was explained to me later in life, teenagers do the things they do because their blood flow is pretty much directed to their reproductive organs, and little gets above their shoulders.

About 10 years later and far from Michigan, I was again in a threatening situation. Single, 25, and a US Naval Medical Officer, it was 1965 at the beginning of the Vietnam War. My ship, the Buchannan, had berthed at the Subic Bay (Philippines) Naval Base for several days. With nothing else to do I embarked on a 3 day shore leave to Manila. The guidebooks suggested Manila was a dangerous place, but that tourists confining themselves to the city center and the waterfront casinos were "generally safe."

Alone in that huge port city, I ventured out my first evening by taxi for one of Manila's plush waterfront casino/show-clubs. The Filipino taxi driver explained in perfect English that his close connections with the US military were the reason I should trust him to select the "best club of all." Aware that the destinations I had chosen were not far from my hotel, I became anxious when were we were still traveling 25 minutes later. We were increasingly distant from the city center and negotiating blighted, dilapidated neighborhoods devoid of any other tourists or foreigners.

My insistent demands to return to central Manila were ignored as we turned into a narrow dirt alley. We stopped at an anonymous, small, grey building with an uninviting, narrow wooden door dimly lit from above by a yellowing incandescent bulb. No color, no sign, no windows, no people. I suddenly felt very isolated and desperately alone in the world. Insisting I just "take a look", my driver opened the door. It was a small bar attended by a scruffy bartender and a few old, rouged "hostesses" perched on bar stools. They all tried to reassure me that I would have "a really good time" there. Several other unshaven, menacing looking Filipino men lounged at a scattering of small tables. The air was stale hot, densely humid and smoky.

Soon my anxiety turned to panic. I started shouting; "I don't want to be here. I want to go back right now." In that critical moment I was not concerned for my own life at all, but only worried that my family and friends might never know what happened to me. I kept thinking I may be about to disappear without a trace.

After several minutes of agitated wrangling, I offered

a bribe to the taxi driver that secured a safe trip straight back to my hotel. By 9 pm my big night in Manila was over: ecstatic, I was again safe, back in my hotel room. Two subsequent Manilla nights there were 'dinner-out/early-to-bed.' My spirit of adventure was thoroughly depleted. 'Lucky again.

GRILL GUY

I WAS A 19-YEAR-OLD PRE-MED JUNIOR at the U. of Michigan in 1958. An easy academic year had me looking for small adventures. I was living in a second floor room above *Madame Kevorkian's Fur Shop* (also her house) on E. Liberty, one of the main shopping streets in Ann Arbor. Across the street was a hole-in-the-wall hamburger joint: "Charlie White's" proclaimed its front window. With no experience and no qualifications, I decided I'd like to be a cook there. I never thought about failing at it.

So, one balmy September day, over a midday hamburger and French fries, I introduced myself to Charlie White with an offer: in exchange for lunch (no pay) I would be his grill guy 2-3 noontimes each week. With few questions asked, he said he'd give me a try. He'd never had help before but probably thought, "not much to lose here."

Charlie was a nervous, jittery little man, around 50, with thinning brown hair and pale skin that wrinkled on his forehead and around his eyes. He was capable of a hearty laugh but possessed a mercurial disposition, bubbly some days, morose others. He had a family but seldom talked about his wife and teenaged son. At one time Charley had been a local celebrity, the owner of a large, popular Ann Arbor restaurant. I learned later that the disease of alcoholism had ruined that. A 10 stools-at-the-counter, breakfast-luncheonette was what he had left.

'Charlie White's' diminutive establishment snuggled against the end of a city block of small stops and businesses —"M-Den News," "J. Leidy Gifts," and "Jacobson's Women's Apparel" among them. The place was only wide enough for a glass-door entrance beside a chest high 5x5' front window, on which Charlie's name was scripted in large, blue letters. Inside on the left, a pale green wall held a cluster of coat hooks near the door; further back, two small tables hugged the wall. On the right a long, speckled grey and white Formica counter accommodated a row of 10 squat, green padded, back-less stools.

My 'station' was behind the counter at its midpoint— standing at a 2x2' flat, greasy grey, aluminum-hooded grill. Always on high, that hot surface emitted an uncomfortable wall of heat, and anytime I wasn't paying attention, it burned another of my fingers. Provisions and restaurant supplies were stacked on metal shelves and in refrigerators and cabinets on both sides of the grill area. Charlie constantly patrolled the back-counter area, taking orders, serving and frequently whacking my butt saying "speed it up, kid."

While demand was greatest for hamburgers, fries, grilled cheese sandwiches and pie a la mode, my repertoire soon extended to Denver omelets, 'Reuben' combinations and ice cream sundaes. The food was very good, but of equal attraction for customers —mostly the proprietors and workers from nearby businesses —was the casual, joking repartee provided largely by Charlie, but eagerly enjoined by me after only a few weeks there. Cooking with my back to the counter-seated patrons, it was easy to be ironic, sardonic and irreverent with many of the familiar personalities, like dignified, dapper John Leidy of the nearby Gift Store and elderly Mr. Krantz in his coke-bottle glasses, owner of M-Den News. After I'd been there a while, in the midst of one barbed exchange, Mr. Leidy remarked; "Charlie, how did you ever find this guy?"

I only worked for Charlie my junior year. The next fall (1959) I began Medical School, graduated in '63, and headed west to an internship in Oregon. I was married and living in Boston when I learned that Charlie died about 10 years after I left Ann Arbor. I suppose now there are few people left to remember him as fondly as I do. I'm indebted to Charlie White and the chance he gave me. My experience with him opened a whole new part of my life; home cooking, culinary study and latter in life, further restaurant kitchen adventures.

When I married Kristin in 1966 I was a pretty good cook, far more at home in the kitchen than she was. That circumstance reversed itself within a year and then persisted about 30 years. I regained home culinary ascendency with my retirement in 2000, which incidentally, was then and continues to be an agreeable arrangement.

Some of my interest in food and cooking rubbed off on my youngest son Jesse. As a boy he often joined me weekends constructing 'restaurant lunches' — experimental food combinations served with creative decoration. As an adult, Jesse graduated from The Culinary School of San Francisco to become a sought-after chef in SF and in Philadelphia for 15 years. Subsequently he acquired a BS degree in Food Science and now heads a team in the test kitchens of the Campbell Soup Company.

I too eventually made it into the Philadelphia restaurant scene in the late 1990's. I began by taking cooking lessons from a famous local chef, Fritz Blank, at his venerable Philly establishment, Deux Cheminee's. I ended up being some-time help in the 'Deux Chem' kitchen, which was long and narrow like Charlie's place, but a lot bigger and busier. I worked Fridays or Saturdays prepping for the evening trade, sometimes also preparing a 5pm dinner for 6-8 waiters and a maître d'. Fritz taught me a lot — from boiling eggs perfectly to butchering a whole calf's liver — with lessons on food science, classical music and 'life' thrown in with the rest. There's a lot to tell about Fritz which will likely end up in some additional legacy pieces.

MEMORABLE MENTOR

IN HIS DOCTOR'S WHITE COAT, he was a short man with a small pot-belly and unruly grey hair that stood straight up. Once, with stethoscope in hand he leaned over a bed-ridden 7 year old, who exclaimed; "Wow, you're funny looking!" The observation was quite accurate; the doctor's mandible was congenitally small and misshapen, resulting in his uncanny resemblance to Alfred Hitchcock. This deformity caused food to enter from the side of his mouth, and spoken words to exit there too, muffled and mushy. Further altered by his thick Hungarian accent, his speech was at first distracting, then riveting. One had to listen carefully to his words, but it was worth the effort.

Dr. Alexander Nadas, a famous pioneer in Pediatric Cardiology and Chief of Cardiology at Children's Hospital, Boston for over 30 years, treated thousands of children and trained hundreds of young physicians there. It takes more than gifted clinical acumen and research skill to successfully head an academic medical department. A few rare department chiefs also lead and inspire by the force of their personalities, expansive wisdom and intelligent good humor. Alex Nadas was one of those.

Modified by wit and irony, Dr. Nadas' huge ego was, in fact, an attractive asset for him. He was an inspired teacher who never relinquished his role as 'The Professor'. On a very memorable occasion, Dr. Nadas and one of his residents became involved in an intense discussion; both had been periodically listening for a year or more to a heart murmur in the young doctor's own child, a murmur produced in that babies' heart by a tiny hole that was slowly closing on its own. Dr. Nadas, after listening that day, insisted that finally the murmur was gone, indicating the hole had closed, but the father was adamant that he still could detect a faint sound. After several exchanges, Dr. Nadas stood to his full 5'7" to declare; "Bill, not only can I hear murmurs when no one else can hear them, but I hear murmurs go away before anyone else hears them go away." This a very funny, nuanced doctor joke.

And could he ever make intelligent and clever use of his adopted English language. I once encountered him agitated and upset by the actions of one of his famous, but vexing, colleagues. "What am I going to do with that prima donna Dr. Van Praagh?" he asked. I demurred; Richard is a highly valuable resource and forbearance is needed." After a moment's thought, he replied; "Well, I tell you Kenny, for a million dollars no one can have RVP., but for a million dollars I don't take another RVP."

Interns and residents gain philosophical and medical knowledge from their doctor peers that is not available in med school classrooms. Dr. Nadas was a fountain of such information. In a hospital conference in which the discussion revolved around the best guidelines for dealing with patients as individuals and humans, Dr. Nadas often offered; "For treating patients and families well, the Golden Rule is a pretty good place to start." I didn't memorize every bit of wisdom he dispensed, but the Golden Rule suggestion stuck.

What else did I gain from this mentor's example? I tried as a doctor to remember his humor, thoughtfulness, confidence and compassion as qualities worth emulating. He wore bright ties with colorful striped shirts. I borrowed some of his look too.

CAMP DOC

I'M IN THE CAMP DISPENSARY contemplating by bloodied face in an old mirror. It's 6 pm on an August day, 1972; the Camp Androscoggin (Wayne, ME) bell is clanging the call to dinner. Roughly 100 boy campers, 12 teen-aged counselors, and 6 senior camp staffers head for the dinning hall. My wife and toddler son Ian too. But not me. I've wounded myself 20 minutes before while imprudently showing off on water-skis. Having taken a spectacular fall, an errant water-ski bonked me in the face, leaving a 2" gash between my eyebrows. I need the camp doctor to "sew it up" (as the kids say) but that's easier said than done. I'm the camp doctor.

Seeing small objects clearly in an old, scratchy mirror is difficult. So is injecting anesthetic between your own eyes. Harder still is needling sutures into your own face, cutting them with tiny scissors, and tying small knots just so: everything in the mirror is backwards, and my brain resists the needed reorientation. In the end the result is satisfactory at best. The residual scar will eventually fade away. I actually emerge a minor camp hero. The campers see me as someone akin to a tough hockey player who gets stitched up after a facial laceration and heads right back into the fray.

Camp Androscoggin, an idyllic introduction to Maine early in our marriage, was a privately owned summer camp for boys 8–15, uniquely situated on a small island in central Maine's Lake Androscoggin. Access was exclusively by motorboat, canoe or other watercraft from the Wayne town dock, just behind the general store and post office.

All the boats belonged to the camp, so getting to/from camp required advanced planning.

Beginning my career at Boston Children's Hospital back then, we had meager resources. An offer arose for a paid, 2-week August 'working vacation' as the doctor at Camp Androscoggin. It was too good to pass up. I had been a YMCA camp counselor and waterfront director summers in my college days. I was eager to get back to that atmosphere — long days of swimming, sailing, hiking, playing team sports. Essentially, being a kid again. Plus, fresh air, free meals and lodging for my small family were included.

Camp Androscoggin didn't disappoint. The food was great, the atmosphere relaxed, and the esprit de corps between campers and staff high. The best part of being there was the little lakeside log cabin provided the camp doctor and family. In particular, it had a snug, screened porch where we slept most nights, dozing off to the mysterious, mournful calls of loons and smelling the pungent scent of surrounding pine trees. No wonder we vowed then to find a place of our own sometime, someplace in Maine.

On our first day at camp, Kristin and I became good friends with Olivier and Laurent, both 20 year old Frenchmen. We were certified Francophiles and they were handsome and roguishly charming. They had signed on as tennis coaches for the camp's duration, a stint they intended to follow with 2 week's travel through New England before heading home to France. As our 2-week August camp service was ending, they realized they had another 14 days before their camp contract was fulfilled, which through their own poor planning left only a few days for post-camp travel. They quietly concocted a plan whereby the Fellows' family would become accomplices in their personal, 2 week-premature, illegal sneak-away. A potential "international incident" was my first thought.

The French 'great escape' went down like this. Before dawn of my family's Saturday morning departure, Olivier and Laurent "borrowed" a camp canoe and stealthily paddled for the Wayne town docks. Lying low in nearby woods until midmorning, they arranged to be hitchhiking about 11am along the little traveled road leading out of town. By prior agreement, my family and I would "just happen" to come driving by, headed back home to the Boston suburbs. How could we be faulted for innocently picking up these 2 hitchhikers who were well known to us? How could we know they were deserters?

Throwing their back-packs in with our luggage, we all proceeded back to Newton where they stayed with us for several days, happily wandering around Boston and Cambridge. They then struck out on their own for a week of sightseeing on the Cape and other parts of New England. Their nefarious plan worked well; they accomplished a tour of the Northeast before flying back to Paris.

No one from Camp Androscoggin ever called to inquire about the coincidental disappearance of their two French tennis instructors on the same morning the camp doctor and family also departed. I'd like to know whether we were even considered suspects in what turned out to be a fairly titillating, artful escapade. Similarly, we never heard again from either Olivier or Laurent. Too bad. I thought I might have been a candidate for a Croix de Guerre or some other French medal.

POST SCRIPT: After reading this story to the Memoir Writing Group, our teacher (RW) suggested it also describes a spirit and sense of adventure in our early marriage.

I think that's true. The camp "fling" led to our long love affair with Maine. Kristin originated the idea of having 4 children, 2 to be adopted. She also pushed me to buy a house in Newton for our young family, and then a "homestead" in Kittery Point. Our momentous move to Philadelphia was instigated by me but propelled by Kristin's enthusiasm for change and new experiences.

We were lucky too: our 'adventures' turned out well.

THE JOY OF RASPBERRIES

Here's the secret to successful raspberry picking: think like a raspberry. They're crafty, deceptive, tricky and shy. Growing in clumps of 5-8, the ripe ones hide behind green relatives to avoid detection. Some — usually the biggest and sweetest — grow solitarily, obscure, down low, among bushy green leaves and thorny stems. Unlike ground-hugging strawberries with their low 'leaf-to-fruit' ratio, raspberry plants grow 4-6 feet tall supported on foliage-dense, crisscrossing, prickly branches. A good picker must lift-up, pull-down, untangle, turn over, separate and inspect from all angles down rows of plants to retrieve the red-seeded prey.

In my 15 yard long raspberry patch, the hunt is further complicated by entwining weeds bearing the same shaped leaves and grey-green color as the berry bushes. They twist round and round the berry canes, adding even more cover for the elusive red fruit. Unwinding the vines enough to pull them by their roots doubles the picking time without increasing the berry yield. It's maddening.

The mosquito provides the berries another defense. My plot supports hordes of them. During the July picking season, green-headed flies join the battle on behalf of the fruit, so I'm forced to pick fruit in the sweltering midday because the vexing insects are less active then. I march into battle under a blazing, humid afternoon sun armored against my airborne enemies. The core of my protection is an airless, black, netted-nylon 'jacket' which covers me head to waist. Covering my face, this jacket prevents the ingestion of belly-berries, a real drawback. Below I wear jeans tucked into tall rubber boots. This is not a cool outfit. It's hot. It's sweaty. Hot head. Hot body. Hot feet. Everything hot, hot, hot.

Of course, I wear a shirt under the mosquito-netting jacket, and dowse myself with Cutter's spray repellent too. The little buggers still find ways to penetrate the clothing and the netting, so no picking session is itch or pain free. People walking along the road just beyond my raspberry rows often comment:

"How lucky for you have berries to pick."

"Oh yes, 'lots of fun" I grumble back.

Forget the impediments; just gathering the raspberries isn't all that easy either. It's a stand-up job, so I hold the collection box in one hand — or precariously cradle it on one bent arm — leaving the other hand free for plucking fruit. But there's a problem; I can become so engrossed in search-and-snatch maneuvers that the partly filled box in my non-picking hand is forgotten, tips downward, and half an hour's work splatters to the ground, irretrievably lost in the thicket. It's not good if someone is walking by at that moment. I don't mutter, I explode in a primal scream of blue language otherwise used by me only in front of a computer.

And have I mentioned the mental stressors in raspberry picking? Deep red berries are the object of the hunt. Purple ones are over-ripe and unusable: yellow-orange to orange-pink ones are tasteless and need to wait for the next picking. But how about those becoming just faintly purple — or those turning 'early red'? Pick now or later? Can I pick again in 2 days? Not if it's raining; not if I'll be busy or away. Almost every picking minute, crucial, stressful decisions have to be made.

If everyone knew all of the personal effort involved and the individual toll taken, they might understand why a commercial half-pint of raspberries is so expensive.

There are rewards for my hours and hours of berry tending; raspberry shortcakes, muffins, pies and especially Kristin's freezer jam, which somehow takes the raspberry to a higher level. On a stormy, cold winter's morning, that jam on warm toast or muffins makes life sustainable. So I'll go on fussing with the plants: trimming, fertilizing, rototilling and watering. And I'll continue picking with all its frustrations and hardships. I've been doing it for 40 years. I know the price.

20ᵗʰ AND SPRUCE

It's a busy midtown Philly corner: no light, just STOP signs. Morning to evening, well-dressed inhabitants from nearby, upscale Rittenhouse Square condos, townhouses and hotels shop its boutiques and fill its trendy restaurants. Dented, rattling white Philadelphia Police cars race westward on Spruce St. and north on 20ᵗʰ, blue lights flashing, potholed chasses bouncing, sirens screaming. Pedestrians and vehicles converge at rush hour, weaving about and around each other with breathtakingly close calls, but rare actual hits.

    Kristin and I rented a 2ⁿᵈ floor condo in a greyed brownstone walk-up just one building — a little restaurant, "Audrey Claire's" — off that corner. Audrey and her cozy place were the intersection's heart and soul. Between Audrey and another downtown eatery owner-friend, Chef Fritz Blank of 'Deux Chem' on Locust St., I had three exciting "restaurant years" in Philly. And who could have guessed that after nearly 35 years of suburban living near Boston and Philadelphia, Kristin and I would find so much fun and such delightful characters in the bustle and complexity of big city life.

    "Oh, sweet, sweet Audrey," sighed Sal my gregarious

Italian barber whose shop was close by on 20th St. While having my monthly haircut, I had asked if he had seen her around the neighborhood recently. He stopped trimming my neck, lowered the comb and scissors to his side, assumed a wistful, faraway look in his eyes; "Aah, Audrey. She's so smart, so beautiful, and so friendly — she must have been a fat girl!"

Most of the men in the neighborhood had a crush on Audrey. A slightly zaftig woman about 30, pretty but not gorgeous with dark hair and complexion, she had alert blue eyes and a persistently pleasant, sincere smile. She had an unselfconscious, comfortable affability: no meter was running on the time or attention she offered. She appeared to have a number of suitors, but no one steady. I presumed she was just more interested in business than matrimony.

Her full name: Audrey Claire Taichman. The namesake restaurant that was her inspiration and her life opened in 1997, about the same time we moved in next door. In short time it became the hippest, busiest restaurant in Philly. The small, dark-wood tabled, galley-kitchen in the dining-room, fresh-flowered vases in open picture-windows establishment energized the neighborhood. Evenings, when owner Audrey wasn't inside attending to her metrosexual foodies and older, establishment regulars, she relaxed on a bench near the front door, happily chatting-up passersby. Eating inside or chatting out front — that's how Kristin, I, Sal, most everyone got to know and admire Audrey.

About once a year I go back to the old neighborhood. After many years I never find Audrey around, even though her original restaurant, plus a newer one across 20th St., are both going strong. She is now a city celebrity, not just a neighborhood icon. There are always several pictures of her in the latest monthly issue of *Philadelphia Magazine* I buy there. She is aging well in her photos, her smile as engaging as ever. 'Hard to believe she still seems to be single.

Sal; such a character too. His barbershop was a converted little storefront with heavily draped windows obscuring the interior: the only peak inside possible through a smudgy glass door missing the usual "Open" or "Hours" sign. A single barber chair occupied the right half of an unpretentious floor space, accompanied by a large wall mirror and a several wall-mounted shelves holding his barber tools, powders, lotions and framed photos of Sal's bocce-playing Italian cronies. It was the left side of the shop that impressed: two L-shaped, tan, high-grade leather couches waited there for the comfort and leisurely lounging of Sal's clientele and intriguing friends.

Sal was in his 60's, short, thin and perpetually smiling under fashionable wire-rimmed glasses and salt and pepper, brush-cut hair. He dressed in trendy patterned T-shirts and contrasting dark slacks, a modest look which contrasted with that of the 2-3 men usually occupying the nearby thickly cushioned furniture. Those middle-aged guys had slicked back, dark hair and sported pinky rings on manicured hands. They were swarthy peacocks in expensive, well-tailored suits and alligator loafers. Over the years I saw them enough to earn a salutatory grunt when we met, but never more than that. And I never saw one of them actually get a haircut.

But I did see this: whenever the phone in Sal's backroom rang, one of those guys quickly ducked through the curtained doorway to answer it. Strain though I did to catch the conversations back there, nothing intelligible ever escaped the mumbling I could only faintly hear. And no consersational clues were ever offered upon retaking their leathered seats. When 'the suits' weren't around, Sal answered the phone and talked in a similar, suppressed tone. Kristin liked to tell friends that I was the only man in Philly who thought Sal's place was really a barbershop. No matter. The haircuts were great.

I retired at the end of 2000 and Kristin and I moved to Kittery Point. The Children's Hospital of Philadelphia held a retirement ceremony and farewell reception for me just before we left, and Sal with wife attended. To me he looked quite uncomfortable in a room full of academics, researchers and physicians, and I wasn't surprised when he skipped out early. A year later when I returned to the old neighborhood at 20th and Spruce, his shop had become a flower store and I couldn't find anyone who knew where Sal had gone. I regret I'll never know what happened to him. And I'll always wonder what business he really was in.

POST SCRIPT: Sal's Italian ancestry was VERY important to him. His bocce team was called "The Italians" (while competitors were "The Irish", "The French" and so on). Some other teams were named "The Notso's" ("Notso Italian", "Notso Jewish", etc.) One summer's day I mentioned to Sal during a haircut that Kristin, proud of her Scandinavian heritage, and I recently had visited a site in Newfoundland where the Vikings, *acknowledged discoverers of N. America*, first landed. Immediately exasperated, Sal threw his hands in the air; "What kind of bull-shit is that?" I told him I was sorry to break his Christopher Columbus bubble. "Don't worry, you can't" he spat.

DEUX CHEM TRILOGY I
Chef Fritz

SOMETIMES HE SIGNED HIS CORRESPONDENCE; "F. C. Blank, Chef de Cuisine et Proprietair (et hoc genus omne), Deux Cheminees'." Other times; "Der Graf Peels Lotsa Potatas." To good friends he was 'Chef Fritz... or just "Fritz"... or "Fr-r-zenpheffer." For loyal patrons his landmark Philadelphia restaurant was just "Deux Chem."

Whether supervising in the kitchen ("taste, taste, taste" his mantra), greeting all patrons at the restaurant's front door, or roaming the dining rooms for tableside conversation, he was the essence of the professional Chef. His round body was dressed in white, head to toe: boxy English Chef's cap, high-necked, long-sleeved smock and shapeless chef's checkered pants hidden under a clean, wrap-around apron. Fritz's large rosy cheeks were so wide that (face-on) you couldn't see his ears. His small, dark eyes sparkled. He had an engaging smile framed by a dark mustache that curved down at the corners of his mouth to join a well-trimmed goatee. Like most cooks, his finger nails were clipped short, his hands chaffed and reddened. But he wasn't always a chef: a lot came before that.

He started as a Pennsylvania drug store 'Soda Jerk'. He later acquired a college degree in Animal Husbandry, eventually becoming a herdsman for 1,600 cows. Then he earned a degree in Microbiology and was appointed Chief of Microbiology at a suburban Philadelphia hospital, a position he held 10 years before he opened Deux Chem in 1978. I didn't meet Fritz until 1997, when I took up cooking lessons at his restaurant.

A large, antique 'Staff Dining Table' occupied a side 'prep' room off the Deux Chem kitchen. Fritz held forth there at lunchtimes, dispensing cooking pearls, culinary history, personal philosophy and classical music trivia (he was also a Trustee of the Philadelphia Singers, the choral arm of the Philadelphia Orchestra.) His noontime guests included singers and musicians, Rittenhouse Park socialites, patrons of the arts, and often another chef or cooking apprentice like me. Sometimes young chefs showed up seeking his approval for a new dish, knowing full well he could be brutally honest. One noon an especially eager, young caterer brought a duck terrine he had been perfecting for weeks. After a slow, tongue rolling taste, Fritz looked him in the eye; "Keep at it, Amigo. This version tastes like liverwurst."

Fritz dispensed kitchen knowledge during lunch and work-breaks at that table, like using any left-over lemon juice to disinfect cutting boards and counter tops. Another: the secret to perfect hard boiled eggs ("oeufs dur") is *cold*... immersion after boiling in an ice bath for 10 minutes. Cooling prevents the sulfurous 'greenish-tinge' around the yolk which Fritz graphically insisted "tastes like dog farts smell." It was there I tried my first Meyer lemon, was introduced to his 'Pennsylvania Dutch' Pickled Red Beet Eggs, and heard about "Touch-of-Grace Biscuits". He liked to tell about his friend, similarly rotund, chef-author Shirley Corriher who, when a girl, cried because her biscuits were not as good as her Grandmother's. "Nanne what did I do wrong?" she asked. She got a hug along with this advice; "Honey, I guess you forgot to add a touch of grace."

At that lunch-table Fritz often revealed details of his personal life: among them, his 25 years of hard-won sobriety from alcohol and his long separation from Neil, his partner who lived in Thailand. Another favorite topic was the cultural history of individual recipes, all compulsively categorized by "food type" (*Fish, Meats, Vegetable sides, Vegetable mains, Desserts,* etc.) and filed in shiny white ring-binders on floor to ceiling shelves next to that table. Most of the recipes began with a paragraph noting its own 'back story' before proceeding to list the ingredients and cooking steps recommended. Fritz approached cooking artistically, scientifically...and academically.

Steeped as he was in French culinary traditions, another pet interest of his was preserving the folk element in N. American food-culture. He staunchly recommended and supported church spaghetti suppers, burned, grilled hot dogs on the 4th of July and (his favorite)... New Jersey Firehouse 'Fried Muskrat Dinners'; "Dr. Ken, you should come with me this weekend. They catch and skin 'em, then deep fat fry 'em. Delicious! Tasty salad on the side; Dixie cup for dessert."

"Oh thanks Fritz, but I think I can't make it this weekend."

Fritz could be 'old school' formal. He often greeted women with a kiss on the hand. He also was casually unselfconscious. In 2001 a giant picture of his face, advertising the "Best Chefs in Philly," appeared on the sides of city buses. He told me that the exposure was good for business, but there was a downside; "Now I have to wear a disguise when I go to an adult book store." Straight-up honest, he never pulled his punches.

I took group cooking lessons from Fritz 1997-98, and then helped weekends in the Deux Chem kitchen doing prep work and staff meals until 2001, when I retired and left Philly. In 2002 my son Jesse, an experienced chef in San Francisco and Ann Arbor, moved back to Philly and joined the Deux Chem kitchen staff for a time. In 2007 Fritz retired to Thailand to join his partner Neil there, and Deux Chem closed. After exchanging biannual emails, contact between us abruptly ceased in 2011. His health was always marginal. In 2014 a friend in Philly sent an obituary from the Philadelphia Inquirer: Fritz died in Thailand the fall of that year, having suffered Alzheimer's disease for some time.

I thought I got to know Fritz pretty well, but he was a complicated man; I always felt there was a lot about him I had missed. I have no idea how he became so thoroughly involved with the classical music scene in Philly... whether he did it for love of the music or just liked the sophisticated people he met there. We never discussed his partner, so I have no idea what he was like, or anything else about their gay lifestyle. He was separated from Neil all of my years in Philly, so his retirement to Thailand was a surprise to me, especially since it separated him from the foods, music and Philly culture he thrived on.

My overall 'take' on Fritz Blank is that he was a generous, gregarious intellectual who enjoyed using his hands in the physical aspects of fine cooking as much as he did the cerebral side of being a great chef — discovering the history of a recipe, refining a classic European dish in modern ways, or in meeting people and pleasing them with his culinary mastery. He enjoyed having lots of friends, but was careful to be forthcoming with only few of them. He loved public acclamation, but spent most of his time alone, listening to music, composing menus, and planning cooking books that never materialized. Maybe that was his defining persona — a man capable of almost anything and interested in just about everything.

DEUX CHEM TRILOGY II
The Restaurant

I WAS 50, and after 20 years in Boston, was being lured in 1987 to Philly by the Children's Hospital of Philadelphia (CHOP). My first recruitment evening there, I was taken to dinner at Deux Cheminees, my hosts hoping to make a favorable impression at one of the city's best restaurants. I was impressed. A menu from that (or any other) evening would include such classics as:
  - Soupe au Pistou, Crème aux Champignons, or Scotch laced She-Crab Cream Soup
  - Salade d'Asperges Grillees , Foie Gras, or Escargots a la Bourguignonne
  - Entrees Tounedos Notre Facon (French brown sauce with Cognac and Madiera)
  - Carre d-Agneau — pour deux (with truffle-filled Sauce Perigord)
  - Canard Roti aux Griottes (red wine sauce and griotte cherries)

Both the restaurant and the food were refined and Old World, neither innovative nor trendy. If I'd been offered a crystal ball that night instead of a finger bowl, I would have been shocked: I'd have seen myself cooking there in the Deux Chem kitchen — just a decade later.

The Deux Chem restaurant resided in a Philly 1880 townhouse listed on the National Registry of Historic Homes. A stately 4 stories, its many windows were bordered in stained-glass and its brick exterior glowed with a red-tan patina. A street level foyer led to a number of Victorian small and medium sized dining rooms lined with 19th Century art and warmed by fireplaces. It exuded a grand style of living, especially when its 15 antique clocks quietly bonged and chimed during the evening. A 'period piece' for sure.

Chef Fritz Blank opened Deux Cheminees ("two chimneys") in 1978. I didn't meet him on my original visit in '87; that didn't happen until 1997. By '97 Deux Chem was celebrated not only in Philly but in the NY Times, Gourmet Magazine and other prestigious publications. Kristin and I had moved from the Philadelphia suburbs to center city in 1997. I'd been 10 years at CHOP and was happily still working there, but anticipating retirement around 2001. In preparation for that milestone I wanted to expand my cooking repertoire, primarily Bistro-style soups, stews, salads, meat and fish entrees. So, in mid-1997 I enrolled in a series of cooking lessons at Deux Chem given by Chef Fritz, then a well-known Philly cook and local character. Another enticement; the restaurant was a pleasant walk down Locust St. from our center city condo.

Gourmet Magazine in an article on "important American Chefs" once described Fritz as "a 300 pound restaurateur from Philadelphia, his arms a mess of tattoos." Indignant, he shot back a letter of protest to the editors of Gourmet; "I have one tattoo on one arm and weigh considerably less than 300 pounds. I am a chef who cooks; I am not a restaurateur… I am a cook. I am a scientist [2 academic degrees]. I am an artist. I am a tradesman." Pure Fritz! Charming, glib, opinionated and uncompromising.

He lived with his old cat 'Bobo' in an enormous

apartment on the floor above the dining rooms. The walls were lined by thick, pine-plank shelves supported by colorful cans of olive oil and other cooking supplies, quite in contrast to the surrounding Victorian décor. Fritz's extraordinary collection of 20,000 cookbooks resided on those unvarnished boards. A visit to Fritz's place was enhanced by the classical music that he continually played there. Desktop, counter, almost any horizontal surface was covered by notes and references for a book he was writing — *The Gastronomy of the Great Composer's: Culinary Lessons of History for Today's Cook* — a prolonged, but ultimately uncompleted, project. But he loved having a New York literary agent to name-drop.

The cooking lessons were held in the Deux Chem basement kitchen, reached from the dining room down a curving flight of stairs leading to a green walled corridor over-hung by a vast array of copper pots and pans of all sizes and shapes. It was my favorite part of the building; colorful, utilitarian and substantive. The kitchen was a widened extension of that corridor; large, black gas stoves and ovens lined one wall, countertops and cabinets the other wall, and in the middle rested a long, narrow island featuring a steam-table for warming ingredients and a butcher-block surface for plating meals. For the cooking lessons, 8-10 students squeezed together on folding chairs on one side of the island, while Fritz lectured and demonstrated in front of us from its other side.

Invariably his teaching was entertaining and useful. True to his academic approach to everything, the lessons were printed out in detail — a list of the entrees to be taught, each followed by a detailed recipe introduced by pertinent historical and cultural notes. Those lessons were all fascinating, some even memorable. Among a host of 'cooking pearls' he dispatched, these are some of my favorites:

- For an omelet, beat the eggs 33 times, never more
- Perfect hard-boiled eggs depend on prompt cooling

in an ice-bath after a precise 8 minute boil (9 minutes for extra-large eggs)
- Authentic Italian tomato sauce contains either onions or garlic, never both
- Substitute sweet marjoram for oregano in sauces to avoid a "pizza taste"
- Classic Salad Nicoise is primarily tomatoes, peppers and cucumbers: tuna or anchovies can be added, but never both (and no cooked veggies, potatoes or eggs)

When in late 1998 I missed a lesson, Fritz invited me to make it up by coming into the kitchen one Saturday morning to help prepare the day's fare. What a kick! From then until I left Philly in December 2000, while still a doctor at CHOP, I often volunteered a Friday or Saturday there, and in the process became an admirer and good friend of Fritz. I also became somewhat of a celebrity among my physician friends for this small foray into life outside the hospital.

In the process, I burned fingers, ruined some food, pestered the staff with questions, got in the way and sometimes helped. I learned that constant tasting is the key to successful cooking and that 8-9 hours of restaurant kitchen work is exhausting.

Cooking gives me an outlet and satisfaction much like watercolor painting: a chance to be innovative, sometimes creative, and to experience a process that is as rewarding as the product. When I'm concentrating on painting or cooking, time disappears and endorphins flow.

Because of Fritz, Deux Cheminees was a 30 year culinary benchmark of excellence in Philadelphia — precisely prepared, classic meals served with stately flare. Fritz retired in 2007. The restaurant closed. Philly lost two icons.

POST SCRIPT: After I retired to Kittery in 2001, a friend who owned Carla's restaurant/bakery in York wanted me to initiate limited-menu (aujourd'hui) dinners there

Thursday, Friday and Saturday evenings. I went so far as to create a comprehensive list of Bistro-style entrees before finally declining the opportunity. I decided I didn't retire from 40 years of medical "on call" to spend my weekends cooking for the public.

Instead, I began taking lessons in Indian cooking from Raj at his Government St. store and tiny eatery here in Kittery, the forerunner of his popular 'Tulsi' restaurant. I then worked for him sporadically over a couple of years helping him prepare Indian food for his market and take-out trade.

History repeating itself in a lesser version.

DEUX CHEM TRILOGY III
FISH PIE AND I

EARLY IN 2000, I WAS PLANNING my retirement in December that year. I'd been a doctor for nearly 40 years, an academic radiologist in Philly for 13 years, and a weekend cook with Chef Fritz Blanc at his restaurant Deux Chemees for a couple of years. I asked Fritz about my inviting about 24 colleagues to a celebratory dinner at Deux Chem, a meal we could prepare together.

Fritz grinned. "Let's do it, my friend." To be really festive, he suggested we make *Coulibiac*, a French version of a Russian peasant dish...actually a complicated fish pie, memorable because of an ingredient called *vesiga* — boiled sturgeon spinal cord.

"Sounds good, Fritz. Find us a Saturday in November."

If I had known then how very difficult Coulibiac is to make, and what an adventure it was going to be, I might have deferred for something else. A recent 2013 New Yorker article on cooking contained this quote from the famous French Chef Daniel Boulud; "I've been trying to make a Coulibiac for 30 years. I have been haunted by it." In the end, this 'culinary tour de force' tormented me too.

Coulibiac is considerably more than a "fish pie." It's the complicated, kitchen equivalent of nesting Russian dolls. To begin, a cooked quail's egg is wrapped in spinach and both are then layered between thick salmon fillets. Next, the egg-spinach-salmon sandwich is surrounded by a sticky mushroom pate. The mushrooms are then wrapped in rice made gelatinous by boiling them with sturgeon spinal cord. Finally, the whole layered cylinder is wrapped in Brioche pastry before baking. Fritz explained that dried spinal cord was no longer procurable, so we would substitute Asian cellophane noodles to provide the appropriate texture and stickiness. He also suggested embellishing the final product with sauce beurre blanc for a truly "lavish touch."

Coulibiac was NY Times' Craig Claiborne's favorite preparation. He requested it for his own retirement party in 1988 at the Four Seasons. French chefs returning to Paris in 1892 after cooking for Russian Czars introduced the present versions of "kolibiaka". The dish became generally popular in Europe in the late 19th Century, then all but disappeared by the mid-20th Century. The big difficulty in its preparation has always been getting all layers perfectly cooked without the juices turning the pastry into a soggy mess. Fritz planned to separate the various layers with thin crepes to contain the problem liquids.

On the selected Saturday in November, Fritz and I began the assemblage midmorning in the Deux Chem kitchen. We were joined by my friend Ed Notebaert, the President of CHOP, amateur cook, dinner invitee, and food groupie who just wanted in on the experience. Since about 24 people were attending that evening, several Coulibiacs were needed. We 3 worked right through the lunch hour, foregoing the usual Fritz-led leisurely noon meal and wide-ranging discussions. The preparation was more fussy cooking, layering, hand primping and shaping then I ever imagined. I was completely exhausted when we finished-up about 4pm and headed for home to nap and dress for dinner at 7. Yvette, Fritz's reliable, mulatto sous chef, agreed to bake the coulibiacs for us later that afternoon.

Refreshed after my nap and a shower, the phone rang about 6pm. It was Fritz at Deux Chem.

"Ken, bad news. Yvette confused some of the oven timers this evening: all of the Coulibiacs, I hate to say, got burned to a crisp."

For a minute I couldn't breathe. Fritz, calm as ever, went on; "I've already obtained Pacific Char (salmon) as a substitute entrée. Don't worry. The dinner will come off fine and on-time with just this 'minor' change in menu."

So there it was. Fritz and I had joined a large number of other chefs for whom Coulibiac was a disaster. Fritz was unfazed. Like the professional he was, he carried on imperiously. Kristin has ever since maintained that Yvette secretly resented my working in the Deux Chem kitchen, and that this 'accident' was 'pay-back.' I've never bought into her conspiracy theory: Yvette and I got along well. But just maybe...?

My guests gathered at 7 in a Deux Chem wood-paneled dining room with fireplace and wall-hung Victorian art. I welcomed the doctors and their wives by informing them they were "winners of a contest they didn't know they were in." They were "my favorite colleagues and friends after 13 years working together at Children's Hospital." Chef Fritz in his welcoming words described how the planned *Coulibiac* had gone up in smoke, and then so gracefully detailed the new menu that no one seemed to care. After dessert, coffee and several testimonials, the guests joined Fritz and me on a tour of the kitchen with its colorful, ceiling-hung, copper pots and pans. After everyone left, I was very relieved: even with a cooking disaster, the evening turned out better than I could have hoped.

I recently found several thank-you notes from that special party. One friend wrote;

"Wow! What an evening. I woke up the next morning needing to sit and relive the events and details of the party — the food, the presentation, the stories, Chef Fritz, tour of the kitchen and mostly the special group of people. This will be one of the memorable events of my years in Philly."

It was memorable for Kristin and me too...a satisfying farewell to my favorite medical colleagues, a story of small scale catastrophe and triumph, and a fitting end to my extraordinary experience cooking at Deux Chem under the tutelage and inspiration of Fritz 'der Graf Peels Lotsa Potatas' Blanc. End of an era.

DON'T HOLD DINNER

FINISHING SOME CLINICAL PAPERWORK at CHOP (Children's Hospital of Philadelphia) one spring evening, I distractedly answered the telephone.

"Dr. Fellows, there's an 11 year old girl here in the ER bleeding severely after a tooth extraction."

"Is this a joke? I'm not a dentist you know."

"No, this is serious. Without packing in her mouth she'd exsanguinate in minutes."

"Okay. I'm on my way."

Alisha was a pigtailed, freckled Pippi Longstocking look-alike, calmly lying in an ER cubicle surrounded by the medical throng a life-threatening problem always attracts.

" Am I going to die?" she asked no one in particular.

"No, you'll be fine" I replied. Although a rather off-hand remark, it had its purpose.

In an emergency situation I avoided getting caught up in the emotion of the moment.

And when other medical personnel where upping their excitement and activity around an emergency, my inclination always was to slow things down — to generate calm.

"What happens if we remove the packing?" I

wondered out loud.

"Just watch." With long forceps the ER attending removed some of the folded gauze pads filling her mouth. Suddenly, a thin, dense stream of red blood shot 2 feet into the room. "Need to see more?" he quipped, repacking her mouth.

"I guess we'd better fix that. Let's get her anesthetized and transported to my procedures' room. I called home.

"Don't wait dinner, Kristin. I have a case that will take most of the night. Sorry."

After seeing the force of the hemorrhage I was certain of the diagnosis and what I needed to do. My thoughts were confirmed by a preliminary arteriogram (an imaging study of Alisha's neck and head vessels); she had a vascular malformation within the (maxillary) bone of her left face. This lime-sized mass of abnormal vessels resulted from a development defect wherein the arteries of her left face joined directly to the veins without any intervening, pressure-reducing capillaries. As a result, the dilated, high-pressure veins had eroded and thinned the maxillary bone around her left upper teeth. When the dentist pulled the loose molar he opened her vascular system to the world—like the proverbial Dutch boy taking his finger out of the dyke.

My task now was, using flouroscopy, to obstruct (embolize) all of the arteries feeding the malformation by threading a tiny catheter from an artery in her groin up into her numerous, small facial arteries, and injecting into each one of them small plastic particles to slow the flow and promote clotting. Few, if any, had ever successfully treated a vascular malformation as complex as Alisha's. My surgical colleagues offered only one alternative for which they had no enthusiasm: a severely disfiguring hemi-facialectomy. Alisha's distraught father agreed to my plan even though he understood the chances for success were unknown.

Assisted by a senior radiology trainee from Texas, we began about 7 pm that evening.

By 3 am we had embolized the feeding arteries from both sides of her face. I elected to stop there, leaving her in a medical coma with her mouth packed for 36 hours. I hoped the slowed flow would entice clotting of the vessels within the malformation. Simultaneously, I was fearful that supply to the malformation might be recruited from arteries in her brain since we had obstructed so many of her facial arteries. Human vessels do that routinely.

A repeat arteriogram on the 3rd day confirmed my concerns; a small artery from her left brain, through her left eye, had reestablished flow to the abnormal maxillary vessels. The bleeding would continue. Cerebral (brain) arteries are not candidates for embolization.

"Well, now what," I mused.

Over a 40 year career, there were many times I was virtually alone — in the middle of the night in a city filled with other medical specialists — and solely responsible for preserving a life. At those times the gravity of the situation is replaced by adrenalin alertness and focused concentration. I remember those moments as real lessons in becoming an adult physician — realizing that often there is no one else, not a parent, not a friend, not a teacher or mentor — no one to help, no one to bail you out.

"Could we ever get some plugs directly into the malformation?" the resident asked.

"Good idea. I've been wondering too," I mumbled. "Let's see."

It turned out to be a cinch. The bone in her left face was so thinned I easily pushed large needles through her left cheek and gums directly into the abnormal vessels. Through them we delivered 12-15 large obstructing coiled-wire plugs. Monitoring arteriograms showed progressive, and finally, complete clotting of the malformation. Good thing; we were all out of tricks.

The skeptical surgeons insisted on taking Alisha to the operating room to extract the packing. They wanted to be able to perform the dreaded excision of her left maxilla if the bleeding had not stopped.

As she left for the OR, I rushed to the airport to catch a plane — medical meetings and lectures were always on my schedule. At the last boarding call, I phoned CHOP.

"Packing taken out. No bleeding. She's already awake and smiling," an OR nurse reported.

"Of course," I replied.

LAGNES DAYS

THE PLACE

KRISTIN AND I INDULGED OURSELVES for 3 years (2005-7) by renting a house in tiny Lagnes, Provence (FR), population 952. Tastefully modernized, our mid-village accommodation was a renovated, ancient farmhouse featuring a winding cement stair to the bedrooms walled by thick cooling stone, and an enclosed courtyard perfect for morning coffee and croissants under the warming Provencal sun.

A 2 minute stroll slightly uphill along our narrow street led to an 'Epicerie' (small grocery store) for pastries and warm baguettes daily...and many choices of cheeses, fresh vegetables and meats if needed. The only other business in the Village Square was the Bar-Tabac, good for newspapers in the morning and a glass or two of Pastis in the late afternoon.

Most days I painted the local scenes with occasional days off for sight-seeing trips in the nearby Luberon countryside. In the attached photo I was painting the Epicerie (not shown) in Lagnes. It was at the end of our last visit there and Kristin was passing by with her camera just as 2 members of a French road-crew came over to view my work. The older Frenchman is smiling reservedly, while his young associate is quite enthusiastic. Mind you: 'thumbs up' in the Roman-Gallic tradition only means "don't throw him to the lions."

THE PAINTING

One cool spring day, while looking for something to paint, I noticed an intriguing pattern of shadows cast on the entrance of the Epicerie. I wanted to capture the light and mood in a watercolor 'sketch', usually a 2-3 hour undertaking for me.

Painting 'en plein aire' in France is rarely a private endeavor. The natives are incapable of passing an artist without stopping to comment. I never understand what they are saying, so I smile shyly and avoid eye contact. When they persist I hasten to explain that I don't speak French, which unfailingly prompts the question; "where are you from?" Intensely wishing not to defend the actions of the US Government around the world, I usually respond; "Je suis Canadian," a small lie that inevitably ends the conversation.

I've painted nearly everything of interest in and around Lagnes. First a drawing, and then the painting (watercolors are a 2 step process) forces me to look at a scene so intently and requires so much concentration, that the details of those places get 'burned' into my memory—the day's weather, the smell in the air, the strength of the breeze, the whole sensorial ambience. It's much more than just the light, colors and shapes that influences a composition.

I spent a summer seeing the great sights and cities of France when I was 16, and many times since. There's no priority now for seeing new places and things. I prefer to find ordinary towns and areas where I can settle in, nose around and get a feel for how people survive there. Painting further strengthens my connection to, and memory of, a locale.

Opinions critical of my artistic abilities are rare when people stop to look and comment. People don't want to be rude. The reaction of the young man in the photo is the most positive judgment I can ever remember. Fortunately, Kristin was there to record the moment.

WALK IN THE RACHEL CARSON WOODS

NO DOGS! $300 FINE! Evander, our one-eared, spiral-tailed Basenji is oblivious to this sign at the start of his favorite trek with me through the Rachel Carson Woods near our house. For him 'Odor-ama' would be a good name for this winding, leaf-strewn trail offering him limitless and irresistible smells of animal DNA. For me it's 'Meditation Alley'...an abiding quiet there, an undulating rhythm of small hills and swales over a forest carpet of muted browns, tans, yellows and greens. The faint creaking of bare oak branches and the soft fluttering of fir trees entices my thought-churning 'monkey-mind' to calm, to retreat peacefully.

After our usual 40 minute meander, the quiet is broken as we exit the woods at the Cutt's Island spillway by cars whizzing by their way to Seapoint Beach. Oh, oh: parked right there is an idling, big white SUV sporting in large green and yellow letters: *"U.S. Fish & Wildlife"* on its doors. But also, its tailpipe is emitting a polluting cloud of exhaust — which jump-starts this instant fantasy:

An uniformed Fish and Game officer ambles my way.

Officer: "Walking your dog in the Rachel Carson Reserve just now?"
Himself: "Well, in court I think it could be called "*res ipsa*" (the thing speaks for itself).
Officer: "Whatever you call it, it's going to be expensive for you."
Himself: "Do you mean that a guy who walks here several times a week, someone who collects loose tissues, candy wrappers and soda bottles, who moves logs, branches and other debris off the trail, who conscientiously stick-flicks his own, and other's, dog poop from the paths into the pucker brush and always keeps his dog leashed to prevent his chasing or abusing wild animals .. you want me to fork over $300 for what is really a victimless transgression?"
Officer; "Yep!"
Himself; " I'm an upright, stalwart citizen of this community, and I'm willing to make a $300 contribution to the work of the USF&W Department here. But I also have one question. Is it federal governmental policy to leave your SUV running when parked?"
Officer: " I don't know about "policy", it's just something we do."
Himself: "Well, I have no enforcement credentials and I'm no expert on local and state statutes. I do, however, happen to know that Kittery has a regulation prohibiting idling engines in parked cars. Now, I'm not going to attempt a citizen's arrest. Let's assume this warning will be sufficient."

The officer, mumbling a few unintelligible words, shrugs his shoulders and walks away shaking his head.
Thus ends another walk in the woods with Evander.
[This partly imagined tale is based on a series of real, separate incidents and facts.]

SYMPHONY HALL ECHO

Back in 1972, Kristin and I attended a Boston Pop's concert to entertain her elderly father Rolla, visiting from California. As Arthur Fiedler began with a Pop's oldie, I glanced at my father-in-law and saw tears streaming down his ruddy face. One life long dream of seeing the Pops was being fulfilled for him, but I thought the emotion was a bit overly romantic.

At that time folk music was for Kristin and me our musical preference and married hobby. We began our listening and playing (she guitar/singing, me autoharp) in the 1960's. It had been Pete Seeger who really attracted me to folk music when I was a college sophomore. Both his music and its messages bowled me over, as much as reading <u>Catcher in the Rye</u> had changed my thinking in high school. I was soon smitten by Mike and Peggy Seeger of the New Lost City Ramblers, Pete singing with the Weavers, and a whole raft of other folk performers familiar to the US House Un-American Activities Committee. I not only thrived on their music and the liberal lyrics, I enjoyed how much my leftist ideas annoyed my conservative parents.

Joan Baez soon became my favorite performer.

Early in our marriage Kristin declared herself severely jealous of Joanie, suspecting that I was actually in love with her too. I did have an extensive collection of Joan Baez recordings; I even was given one of her albums by a grateful patient when I was an intern, some indication that my infatuation was not subtle. I also acquired many more favorites as a married young adult...Woody and Arlo Guthrie, Kris Kristofferson, Emmy Lou Harris, and Gordon Bok among others. Their music both amused and inspired me. I haven't kept up with contemporary music at all, but I do have all of those old performers on CD's and play them daily while painting in my studio. I never tire of the listening.

Some months ago, after a long hiatus, Kristin and I returned to Symphony Hall on a blustery cold winter's night. It was packed mostly by seniors like us, 'come to hear two folk music legends. First to perform was Kris Kristofferson, still tall in jeans but bent now, his craggy face indistinct behind a wispy white beard. He performed alone for nearly an hour, singing his familiar, self-composed songs in a distinctive growl grown weaker and creakier, but retaining all the emotion, intensity and humor of his younger days. I was in personal lip-synch heaven.

The star attraction of the evening was Joan Baez. It was the first time I had seen her in person, and even before she sang I was smitten again. On the huge, dim stage, a single spotlight lit up her bobbed, steel-grey hair and her dark, Latina face. Her graceful figure in black pants and black jacket over a simple white blouse was accented by a knee length vermilion-red scarf and the large, yellow-tan guitar in her hands.

Her performance was indelible. Singing a mix of new material and old songs, her soprano voice and poetic phrasing soared; "had a dog and his name was Blue —here-r-r-re Blue-u-u-ue...you good do-o-g,...you."

Her pure sound reverberated throughout the stilled auditorium. Time had stolen no strength from her voice and no poise from her stage presence. On and on it went, 'Banks of the Ohio', 'Joe Hill', 'Farewell Angelina', 'Silver Dagger', each song bringing thunderous applause. I wanted it to go on forever.

Also, when no one was watching, I dabbed away a few tears, not minding if anyone might consider them a 'bit overly romantic.'

ONE OLD TRUCK

"How old?" says a geezer heaving his trash bag on the accumulated pile.
"1940. 2 years younger than I am," I reply.
"She's a beauty. I just love old trucks like this" he smiles.
This is a frequent conversation I have at the Kittery Dump while unloading my relic Plymouth pickup. I always wonder at the attention it attracts. Is it nostalgia? A general fondness for antiques? Whatever the motivation, many old men and a few senior women can't help but admire my vehicular echo of the 'good old days.'
The truck's body is a formidable sculpture in metal dressing up a durable piece of machinery. My first car as a teenager was a 1934 Plymouth Coupe — a hand-me-down from my grandfather. That car too was a fortress. In the mid 1950's a contemporary Ford sedan crashed it from the rear, the Ford suffering a crumpled grill, hood and motor. The coupe was virtually unaffected. After 74 years of use, my truck is still rust free and nearly undented. Amazing.
And it has character. It is a lustrous black — very, very

black — with a shiny chromed grill, front bumper, hood ornament, and hub-caps. "PLYMOUTH" embossed in bold red, capital letters extends across the tailgate. Out-sized, curving front and rear fenders identify its 1930-40's style, along with round-edged running-boards and a tall, similarly rounded-off cab. Perched on each front fender, big, bullet-shaped headlights stare forward, creating a 'humanoid' look, one now featured in Disney's car and truck cartoon movies.

If you could jump in, behind the thin steering wheel with its small central horn button, you would sink unevenly into a red-brown bench-seat with bad springs. A '4-on the floor' stick-shift lever would nudge your right leg. Through the spokes of the steering wheel you could make out a simple, black dash-board featuring only a round speedometer flanked by small, square gauges for fuel, oil pressure, and temperature, none of which work any more. When purchased 14 years ago, the speedometer functioned, but recently its red arrow tired of spinning and just fell off. No matter: with a top speed of 35 - 40 mph it's unlikely to ever concern the Kittery Police. Far to the right there's a quaint little glove compartment, non-functional until rebuild in dark wood some years ago by my handy Danish brother-in-law.

Surprisingly, the truck's cab is "air-conditioned". In the middle of the dashboard there's a small, chrome handle. Twist it clockwise and the bottom edge of the entire windshield tilts outward, letting in a cooling breeze. Still too hot? Open it further, go a little faster. No Freon. No maintenance. Simple. Effective.

There's a short, single wiper blade on the driver's side of the windshield. Operated by a vacuum pump, when activated it makes one ineffective sweep, then needs to rest before a return swipe can be requested. I don't take the truck out on rainy days.

The original motor was reconditioned and runs like a sewing machine... a loud one.

The motor is a 'flat-head six, whatever that means. It roars and growls while the springs squeak and whine, the doors rattle, and the whole truck creaks and moans. It doesn't offer a peaceful ride. The brakes are weak so constant vigilance is required to avoid sudden stops... this truck isn't capable of sudden stops. It steers like a little red wagon — loose and bouncy even on the best of roads. In a car magazine its road handling would be rated "highly dangerous." That's the reason I only drive it on clear, dry days and let it hibernate in my garage from November 'til May.

Shifting gears requires a technique called "double clutching." It's an acquired skill necessitating considerable practice. Performed imperfectly, it produces a dense metallic, grating and crunching of gears. In my early experience the guys at the Kittery Point gas station used to yell; "Hey, grind me a pound" as I pulled away from the pumps.

Every now and then I'm requested to bring the old truck to a fair, auto show or fund-raiser. The most memorable outing was a couple of years ago when York, ME celebrated the reconstruction of its old, wooden Sewell's Bridge with a parade of antique vehicles. My granddaughter at 5 and I drove in the parade, Ella in the passenger seat smiling and offering a 'Royal wave' (Queen Elizabeth style) as taught her by her grandmother. A picture of us in the truck was published next day in the Portsmouth Herald. You can look it up.

Both the old Plymouth and I were born without odometers. Neither of us really knows how far we've traveled. Who knows how far we might go? Like the Grateful Dead's "Do-dah man", we "Just keep truckin' on"...fade-in...

Sometimes the lights all shining on me;
Other times I can barely see.
Lately it occurs to me...
What a long strange trip it's been.

ROGER AND I

"Thank goodness, thank goodness it's not his pitching arm" moaned his distraught wife.

"Ah, actually it *is* his pitching arm," mumbled the ER resident.

The patient, Roger Clemens, the famous Red Sox pitcher sat between them, rather bewildered. Could he pitch again this season? In the upcoming World Series? Was his career over?

Fall, 1986. Roger was throwing a season ending game for the play-off bound Red Sox when a line-drive smashed into his right forearm. Whisked from Fenway Park to Children's Hospital just a few blocks away, he was in the X-ray Department where I worked. Red Sox players commonly came there with their injuries because one of the team's owners was also a Children's Orthopedic Surgeon. I met a lot of the players and was always impressed how concerned they were about their bodies and any injury, however trivial. Their physical well-being was their lively-hood, and it was easy for them to 'catastrophise' any thing physically amiss. I met them, talked to them, took care of them, but never asked for their autographs.

When Roger and his semi-hysterical wife arrived that evening, I wasn't there or even on-call. Dr. Jane Share, one of our best Radiology Residents, was on duty and supervised the imaging of Clemen's valuable right arm. Not a fan herself, she was working days with me then and knew I was a Red Sox fan. It was she who described to me the following morning, Mrs. Clemen's confused ranting about the contused arm. She also added this feminine detail; "You should have seen her. Roger's wife came straight from the ball park wearing a gold satin dress and stiletto heels!" Dr. Share, a serious young doctor from a conservative Texas family, thought that was just too much.

Radiographs of Roger's arm showed no fracture or other serious injury, information that didn't lessen his pain or concern. Dr. Share related she desperately wanted to get his autograph for me, but was inhibited by his celebrity and discomfort. Finally overcoming her reticence, she asked; "Roger, could you possibly pen an autograph for my boss?"

"It's my writing arm that's hurt, ma'am," he replied. "How about *you* write something and I'll sign it?"

So she did. The next morning Dr. Share handed me a copied x-ray of Roger Clemen's pitching arm bearing this inscription:

"To Ken Fellows — from one legend to another — Roger Clemens"

I thought it was hilarious... a clever, ironic "autograph" showcasing Dr. Share's sense of humor. No so my wife. Dr. Share was an attractive young woman whose marriage at the time was shaky. Kristin had frequently expressed concerns then that Dr. Share was in love with me. Despite my protests to the contrary, she took this vignette as supporting evidence. *Disclosure: whatever motive and emotions she had, Dr. Share's connection to me was entirely hospital-based and completely professional.*

That autograph is now almost 30 years old. I once hoped it would become a valuable collector's item, perhaps expensive enough to fund my retirement. Unfortunately, later in his baseball career, Clemens encountered a number of legal problems including a charge of lying to Congress. Although the accusations against him were never upheld in court, his reputation was sullied. With his memorabilia now severely diminished in value, all that that remains is an old, copied x-ray and a pretty good story.

KERALA
Bombay, 1980

At 2 am in a dim, sweltering, airport customs hall, I was stuporous... a sleepless, 20 jumbo-jet hours from Boston. A grim Indian official grabbed my passport and luggage and disappeared. Warned this would happen, I was still anxious. The cavernous, grey-cement airport teemed with confused tourists and hustling baggage totes. The humid air reeked of sweat and curry. I was overwhelmed... as if dumped on a strange planet, disoriented and alone.

An hour later, still dazed and reeling but reunited with my belongings, I chose a rickety black cab — one of hundreds being hawked by frantic, shouting drivers — and headed for the Bombay International Hotel. Pulling into dense city traffic, the trip became nightmarish. In hazy, yellow-grey streetlight, a side-window 'slide show' evoled: flashing images of humans in rags, creaky wooden carts, scrawny cows and rickety bicycles. A horn-blaring, brake-jamming maze of scrambling people and battered vehicles. When we stopped, the scene worsened: out of nowhere, severely deformed bodies, emaciated adults and sullen children begged at the car's doors. Amputated and twisted limbs — clouded, unseeing eyes—naked, starved babies—were thrust at me in bewildering succession. Completely undone, I eventually staggered into the Intercontinental Hotel and collapsed in a lobby chair. What had I done? How could I cope with this unimaginable, frightful place?

The hotel was an oasis of Indian graciousness with its contemporary décor, ubiquitous potted flowers, clean, colorful rooms and pleasant, helpful staff. A needed place to recover. The American Heart Association had sent me to Trivandrum , the capitol city of the state of Kerala at India's southern-most tip. For a month I was to teach the diagnosis of congenital heart disease at a University Heart and Neurological Institute. During this short layover in Bombay, I tried to adjust to the myriad families eating and sleeping on the streets, gutters and sidewalks. Two days later, boarding a southbound plane for Trivandrum, I worried how Kristin, who was coming to join me in a few weeks, was going to navigate what I had just endured, even though someone planned to meet her and guide her introduction to teeming India.

Kerala was a sunny paradise of palm trees, wide beaches, bright colored saris and green cities and towns. My accommodation was at Kovalum Beach Resort, a 30 minute drive from Trivandrum. The low, tiered, 'Danish-modern' hotel stepped down a gentle slope to wide black-sand beaches. Each room offered panoramic views of the Arabian Sea and its stunning red-orange sunsets. From my balcony I looked down on a busy fishermen's beach — a jumble of small boats, men drying and mending nets, women sorting fish, and kids darting around from the water's edge to the palm jungle at the inland border of their sandy world. Mornings I awoke to the rhythmic chants of those fishermen folding their nets before putting out to sea in one-person, shallow canoes carved from split tree trunks. Later in the morning, women emerged from thatched shacks among the palm trees to gossip in small circles while pounding tapioca root, the mainstay of the local diet... a scene probably centuries old.

Daily I was driven to the Heart Clinic, a clean, new hospital on a green university campus in Trivandrum. Recently built in modern design, it was well staffed by young doctors with the latest equipment who were eager to learn. Those half hour trips were an ever changing pageant of exotic flowering plants, meandering cows, road-building elephants, and frenetic people. Groups of smiling, high-school and college women in multi-hued cotton saris sauntered along the road-sides. Their colorful clothes contrasted with their long black hair and accented their dark eyes and healthy white teeth to create focused images of beauty emerging from the street dust and exhaust haze. Pairs of men walked there too, earnestly talking while absent-mindedly folding their tan, split-front 'lungi' skirts up...and then down...then up...then down...in a repetitious, natural choreography.

Parts of those trips were scary. My Indian driver was a swarthy, young man who loved speed. The narrow, winding, unpaved roads were always crowded by preoccupied pedestrians, assorted conveyances and various animals. Cringe-worthy near misses occurred regularly.

On one of those daily, chauffeured adventures, the drama elevated. Midmorning we were weaving through the local chaos, when suddenly a glaring, uniformed policeman stepped in front of our car. With a baton, he waved us through a gated wall into a dusty, packed dirt courtyard, its square space rimmed by low-slung, tan buildings with barred windows. The gate slammed shut behind us. We were locked in a local police compound. No explanation given; no English spoken.

The officer pulled my driver from the front seat and into an unmarked building. I was left sitting and sweating in the backseat—perplexed and worried. An hour passed. I again felt isolated —-much like my anxious arrival at the Bombay Airport weeks before.

Finally my driver reappeared, downcast and sullen. The gate opened and wordlessly we drove on to the Clinic. Several days later I learned my driver had struck a bicyclist on his way to fetch me that morning, and the police were waiting to arrest him on our return trip. He apparently got off with only a fine. Nothing more was said. And nothing so unnerving happened again.

Kristin arrived near the end of my assignment to spend a week in Kerala with me. She too came to love South Indian food, landscape and culture. But she didn't find everything easy or pleasant. Her arrival in Bombay had been as traumatic, as other-worldly, as mine. The couple responsible for meeting her at the Bombay airport had failed to find her there. She was forced to negotiate her own way through Bombay to the hotel. Alone and frightened, she spent most of her first 24 hours there discouraged and in tears. Despite the exotic beauty abundant in India, even later she could not suppress her shocking introduction in India. I understood completely.

STAIRWELL LESSONS

AROUND 5 AM ON WINTER MICHIGAN MORNINGS you could find me, age 12, and 3 other boys sitting inside on the bare wooden steps of a long, unlit stairway trying to get warm and stay awake. We were paperboys. The Grand Rapids Herald truck bringing our packs of papers was often late — delayed by Lake Michigan snow squalls dumping another 6-8 inches. We 4 were lucky to have the shelter. Squeezed between Huizinga's Drug Store and Harm's Barbershop, the old stairs led to a second floor apartment. Out of pity, the occupants left the stairwell's door unlocked as a refuge for us.

I trudged 20 minutes through the drifts and over black ice just to get there those mornings. After the bundled papers were heaved to the curb around 5:15, we boys brought them in and began folding each paper before loading our grey canvas shoulder bags with "paper missiles" to be thrown on customers' lawns, walks and porches. *Except me.* My father insisted I place the newspapers behind each customer's storm-door or under a doormat. That meant I walked farther, worked harder and took longer than the other guys. Which was his point: by doing more than they did, I would be more successful — attract more customers — receive bigger tips.

I delivered 33 daily papers (38 on Sunday) to small,

middle class '50s homes over a 5 block area. The time required depended on the weather, but it usually took an hour or more. Since the Sunday editions were 4 times heavier than the dailies, my father helped, ferrying them in the open trunk of his car as I made my rounds. I didn't imagine then that 20 years later, in Newton, MA, I would be lending the same 'Sunday morning assist' to my own 4 children on their paper-routes.

As a preadolescent, I learned early the value of money. In my business I bought the newspapers for $.20 and sold them for $.25. Plus tips, I earned about $15 a week, enough to keep me in Clark bars and drugstore 'phosphate' sodas while also saving for my first big-ticket purchase, a Columbia racing bike. Once a month I met my customers face to face. With a shiny metal coin changer strapped proudly to my belt, I marched door-to-door collecting for payments due. To encourage generous tipping, I perpetuated an engaging smile and boyish demeanor as soon as the front door opened.

As successful entrepreneurs must, I became a keen student of human character and behavior. Despite appearances of moderate affluence, customers' responded to my collecting unevenly. Consistent generosity lived next door to confirmed stinginess. Saints and four-flushers all on the same street. My clients could be sorted into 3 groups; big-tipping bill payers, conscientious non-tippers, and a few non-paying/non-tippers who never answered my knock, couldn't find their purse, or only railed about the Herald's editorial page. I became a severe critic of people back then. Years later, I'm less judgmental. Well, sort of.

An exciting part of my monthly collections was anticipating that at the last house on my route, Marilyn King might answer the doorbell's ring. She was the reigning Home- Coming Queen at Ottawa High School. Most boys in Ottawa Middle School considered her the ideal of feminine beauty — tall, smiling, blue-eyed and blond. My secret fantasy of actually meeting this goddess was never fulfilled. Which is just as well: I probably would have been struck dumb or stuttered myself into a quick, whimpering retreat off her front stoop. And anyway, her mother was a gracious big-tipper.

A classmate of mine, Mary Jane Boyles, lived in a house near the start of my route. I had a crush on her and always hoped for an encounter when collecting. Then, in 7th grade, a tragedy occurred: her father ran a hose from his car's tailpipe to its interior. It was the first suicide, probably the first parental death, any of us had known. How could I face Mary Jane, or her mother, at collection time? Could I be stoic? What could I possibly say? I had no answers, so I took the easy way out. I made a 'business decision:' I stopped collecting at her house for months. Mentally I wrote off the losses as "a memorial contribution." When I eventually resumed my collecting, enough time had passed and there was no longer need to revisit the devastating event. But, I've always regretted the copout it was.

My granddaughter is bemused by my descriptions of delivering newspapers. For her it's all in the past tense. Only adults in cars deliver papers anymore, and the very papers are on a path to extinction. Who needs them when computers provide updated information every few minutes? Well me; I still need the papers along with my morning coffee. I find getting news from a computer awkward and uncomfortable despite its timeliness. It reminds me too, that 'every time we get something we want, we give up something we had.'

Uncomfortable, hard work builds character while teaching the value of money, a business obligation teaches responsibility, and doing more than is expected is a way to get ahead in the world. Those were the life lessons incubated in that cold Michigan stairwell of my youth. In turn, I passed those ideas on to my children who, as adults, have thanked me for providing the advice. I've usually accepted credit for the guidance, while simultaneously thinking they really should thank their grandfather.

THANKS, DEWITT

Hey, Dewitt. Among the unforgettable characters in my life you are a favorite. Humorous, entertaining, gifted and wise, you awoke some creativity in me while making painting engrossing and fun.

It was my wife Kristin who put me on to you. She took one of your watercolor classes and recognized in you a teacher likely to suit me perfectly — a provider of explicit direction, a prescribed approach, and unflinching, ironic criticism. My kind of guy. In my very first class, you stopped at my easel to view my early progress. You announced to the whole class, "Ken, at this point in that painting you could have done 3 things wrong. You did all 3!" I smirked: a perfect score my first day.

I wasn't at all put off by your curmudgeonly comment. I tend toward the grumpy myself. Your 'clear wash' technique, emphasis on perspective, and encouragement to 'paint boldly' (to avoid the washed out hues of little old ladies and fussy bachelor uncles) jumpstarted my enthusiasm and hastened my progress. My draftsmanship, pretty weak to begin with, improved as I copied your detailed under-drawing.

I started Dewitt Hardy classes 15 years ago. Recently

retired then, I wanted to paint in the worst way—and I did. Many years of pre-retirement painting instruction in Philadelphia had done little more than instill some basics. At one time I considered burning all my paint brushes the evening a young instructor at the Philadelphia College of Art proclaimed we would be painting cats for several sessions. Paint cats! 'Not something I could ever do. It's a miracle I persevered.

Your instruction from the start was clear and intense, particularly when you were teaching how to paint nudes with watercolors. I was intrigued, even amused, by the very specific steps you demanded in painting the human figure. A favorite moment came at the end of a figure painting session when an impudent fellow student challenged you:

"Come on, Dewitt. There's lots of ways to paint the nude. We don't have to do it your way, do we?"

You spun around and leaned over the middle-aged provocateur. Pointing your index finger in his startled face, you growled,

"Yes you do! And I'll tell you why. If you go home and paint the nude your way, you will get confused… and then you'll get frustrated, and finally… completely discouraged. You will then give up painting…and then you will… die!"

I have immortalized that moment in its retelling many times: I like to call it *Dewitt's Theory of Artistic Mortality*.

Someone hearing all this might assume you are a large, imposing, man. In fact you are physically and sartorially distinctly unimposing—squinting and bespectacled, short with an athletic shuffle (from your baseball and hockey playing days), gray hair perpetually covered by a beat-up baseball cap, and less than regal in cut-off sweatshirt, thread-bare jeans and battered tennis shoes. I love how you attend your public art receptions similarly dressed, just as you would for any day of painting or holding a class. Pretentious you are not.

I also admire how you have made a living from art alone: from your painting, classes and instruction. Beginning as a gifted drawer in childhood, you have risen to have your paintings collected by large museums from NYC to San Francisco. In this Seacoast region you are a legend: the acknowledged master of watercolor.

For someone so revered, when I look back on my 8 years in your classes and workshops, I should have been more respectful: more serious and less willing to 'jerk your chain' now and then. I only did it because your ego is so strong, and your cranky persona tempered by such a good sense of humor. And I thrived as an object of your signature gruffness... like the time the well-known local painter, Dustin Knight, came to our class to expand her watercolor skills. She was retiring and modest, but you shocked me by your attitude toward her — so deferential, so obliging, so conciliatory. Unable to contain myself, I blurted,

"I can't believe what I'm hearing, Dewitt. You just said that she can paint however she wants to — do whatever she wants! What?...she doesn't have to follow the script,...not adhere to the Hardy Method? Am I in a time-warp here?" You answered;

"Of course she can do as she likes! She's a talented, widely recognized artist — not some *schlemiel* like you."

Snickering quietly, I again basked in the glow of another unambiguous assessment.

And there were still other 'public evaluations' I elicited. In 2 separate classes, when I was somewhat provocative, in frustration you offered the firm opinion that I was "an asshole." I'm really fond of those moments. Their memory always makes me smile.

Dewitt, thanks for mentoring my late years in watercolors. Your advice and example have been indelible: whenever I'm painting now, I hear your voice in my head—sometimes encouraging, more often groaning, at what I've done. You were the teacher for me—limitlessly knowledgeable and entertainingly sardonic.

AT SEA

JULY 1, 1964, I FINISHED MY INTERNSHIP in Portland, Oregon and, ordered by the US Navy, headed directly to San Diego to become a Naval Medical Officer. In 3 weeks at the Naval Base Training Center I learned how and whom to salute, the strict Navy protocol for boarding a ship, and how my lineal service number defined Naval command hierarchy (the officer with the lowest number has seniority, and therefore 'wins' any discussion). My assigned ship was the USS Buchannon, a 'super Destroyer' carrying 250 men and the lead ship for a ship squadron composed of 3 other Destroyers having 150 men each. The Navy owned me for the next 2 years. I was eagerly anticipating visits to Asia and other exotic parts of the Pacific. We weren't at war. Everything seemed rosy.

I first went to sea that October. On orders from the Pentagon, the Buchannon steamed from San Diego to San Francisco to represent the military at a U. of California v. Naval Academy football game. Desperately sea sick for 2 days, I recovered enough to marvel at sailing into S.F. Bay under the Golden Gate Bridge while fireboats arched wide plumes of spray over the ship. The 'old salts' told me anyone prone to *mal de mer* will suffer every time they head out. My experience confirmed that. But the illness is self-limiting and compensated by so much else at sea: the kaleidoscopic colors of sea swells, the extended silver shimmer of moonlight on water, swooping fights of seabirds, wave-skimming flying-fish, the reassuring vibration of propellers in the curl of the ship's wake, and the mingling smells of wet sand, sea-weed and salt-air. Even a stoic can be seduced and enchanted.

I was seasick again in December as we began an 9 month deployment to the Western Pacific. Our mission was to cruise the length of Indonesia to challenge its newly declared 200 mile territorial limit. I was concerned the provocation might disrupt my anticipated leisurely ocean cruise to Australia, Japan, Korea and other ports. Well, something did happen, but not what I, or anyone else, expected.

Just as we neared Indonesia, another US warship, the Maddox, reportedly took fire from a North Vietnamese boat — an incident that escalated a regional conflict into "the Vietnamese War" (1964 — 1973). The Maddox quickly withdrew and the Buchannon ordered to replace her. So began my 6 months of going in circles in the Gulf of Tonkin, a small body of water uncomfortably defined by the enemy shores of N. Vietnam to the west and "Red China" (its name then) to the north and east. Our prospects were not good. I was apprehensive. We were the only ship there: the rest of the fleet (an aircraft carrier and 3 destroyers) remained hundreds of open sea miles to the south. Our primary mission was to pick up US fighter pilots who needed to ditch their planes after being shot-up over N. Vietnam. Our purpose was noble, but our ship highly vulnerable.

The Buchannon was practically incapable of protecting itself in the shallow waters of the Tonkin

Gulf. The Bath, ME made destroyer was designed for antisubmarine warfare. There was no such threat in the Tonkin Gulf which averaged only 20-30 feet deep. The enemy there used small patrol boats and converted sampans mounted with large caliber machine guns to attack. In the grand military tradition of 'SNAFU' the Buchannon had no machine guns or other weapons effective against small surface vessels. I never felt safe there, but fortunately no enemy ever fired at us in the 6 months I was on board.

The ship did have an anti-aircraft cannon protruding from a large, revolving turret on its bow, just in front of the bridge where the ship's steerage and command operated. The turret sported a clear, 'observation bubble' on top. The sinister cannon's barrel was 5" wide and 15 feet long. Monthly we practiced shooting it at kite-targets towed a hundred meters behind a crewed airplane. I was assigned on those occasions to be the "safety officer" — the guy who sat in the bubble and squeezed a switch *only* if the gun's cross-hairs were on the target drone, not on the manned plane. This simple job was scary: firing the first round created a dense cloud of smoke that enveloped the bubble, completely obscuring the target and all else. The gun kept shooting' blam, blam, blam...while I had no idea where it was pointed. My naive trust in 'fail-safe' technology was mercifully rewarded. Although I was always on edge doing that job, no accidents occurred.

Of course, I was the ship's doctor too, but I had little to do medically those sweltering S. China Sea days. Most injuries and illnesses were minor among the generally young and middle-aged men on board, and there were 2 medical corpsmen to treat them. I did minor surgery (drained abscesses, excised skin cysts) and handled a few emergencies. One was talking a distraught, 19 year old seaman dangling from the ship's stern, out of suicide. Another was consulting over ship-to-ship radio with a corpsman on a distant destroyer about how to revive 5 sailors unconscious from heat stroke (all survived, although one needed intra-cardiac medical injections). My biggest test was a seaman with acute appendicitis needing surgery. One possibility was to turn the officer's mess into an operating room with the patient on the dining table and a temporary surgical light inserted above it, a shaky, alcoholic senior Corpsman as the anesthesiologist, and a 20 year old junior Corpsman as my assistant. The alternative was to convince the Captain to steam 6 hours to the south to an aircraft-carrier staffed by real surgeons and operating rooms. The carrier option prevailed. The young sailor survived. Curiously, in all my time in the Tonkin Gulf, we never had to pick up a downed pilot which was the reason the Pentagon had us there in the first place. In summary, being a doctor at sea comprised mostly languid hours and days, punctuated by occasional moments of adrenalized stress.

Having so much leisure time, I found other things to do. Anticipating a residency in Radiology after my 2 year Navy stint, I did a lot of medical textbook reading and memorizing.

I also volunteered as the ship's newspaper publisher and travel writer. Having access to the shop's teletype machine, I produced a 4 page ship's newspaper every few days. The sailors liked reading it and its compilation occupied some spare hours. After every 4-5 weeks of circling the Gulf of Tonkin, we traveled to Japan or the Philippines for a few days of 'R&R.' Using the ship's limited library and my own collection of travel books, I wrote travel brochures for the crew and officers. In 5-6 page booklets I previewed sites of interest, cultural details, and available recreation in our destination port — knowing well that the waterfront bars and local women were the sailors' preferred attractions. Lacking effective moral or religious arguments against such diversions, I inserted advice on how to avoid venereal diseases and their long-term consequences. In general, the sailors found my efforts more quaint than persuasive and more presumptive than useful.

The Buchannon's commanding officer, Capt. Sam Orme, became a sage uncle to me during that voyage. Short, grey haired over thick bifocals, in his late fifties and nearing retirement, he was personable, intelligent, and funny — a chain smoking, alcoholic, lapsed Utah Mormon who often called me to his stateroom in port to treat a hangover or prescribe *prophylactic* antibiotics, and at sea to discuss world events and reflect on the human condition. Most of his advice was prefaced: "Well, doctah..."

"*Well doctah, my wife really appreciated your clinic for the ship's families back in San Diego, and especially your taking care of her various problems. As you may have noticed, my wife rather enjoys ill health.*"

"*Well doctah, be sure to marry a woman who has interests in life other than raising children. Otherwise, an empty nest is an unhappy place.*"

"*Well doctah, people back in the US always support a war like this at its beginning. They like to see their tax-financed new weapons put to use. But when dead American boys start arriving back home, that attitude will change, and the war will become highly and increasingly unpopular.*" I didn't have any idea then how prophetic this was.

Capt. Orme always reminded me of James Cagney's cranky ship's captain ("Well now, Mistah.....) in the movie 'Mr. Roberts." That may be a reason why our ship's junior officers, most recent graduates of Annapolis, and I loved to reenact scenes from that movie — where on balmy, tropical evenings the kindly ship's doctor, puffing his pipe, casually strolls to the ship's bridge to dispense philosophy, wisdom and droll humor. At other times we shared many raucous evenings in the Naval Officers' Clubs in the Philippines and Japan. Some strong male bonding happened in that short, intense time aboard ship. I often wonder how their careers and private lives ever played out.

I was ordered back to the US after 6 months while the Buchannon remained in the Tonkin Gulf for months after. I rode back on a small destroyer where I shared a tiny stateroom with a geeky, young Naval officer I didn't much like. When I told him I was headed for duty at El Toro Marine Corps Air Station, he suggested Laguna Beach would be the best place for me to live. He casually suggested the name of a girl — Kristin Thorsdale — he had once blind dated and who lived in Laguna.

"You should look her up." So I did. We clicked. We've been married 50 years.

The return trip on that old destroyer seemed endless: the waves tossed it around like a beach ball: it was slow, I was an interloper, and my cabin was hot and cramped. One day, after 2 weeks of misery, I stepped on deck to discover a miracle: the pungent smell of land. When you've been at sea for a time, long before you can see land, you can smell it — the greenness of trees and grass, the heat of scorched earth, the exhaust of vehicles and the fumes from smoke stacks combine to alert the senses. Welcome back! Small wonder sailors and astronauts bend down and kiss the ground first thing after returning from a long voyage.

'SISTER C'

HER SUV CREPT UP MY DRIVEWAY a recent hot, July morning. I was on the lawn refinishing porch furniture. Rolling down her window, I expected a "how do I get to Fort Foster?" Instead, a solitary, small, bespectacled woman of about 40 asked in a hesitant voice; "Are you Ken Fellows?" That's how simply this contemporary fairy tale began.

I answered I was Ken and asked what she needed.

She offered that her real name was Elise F., but everyone called her 'Sister C.' She explained that she lived across Chauncey Creek from me and some days ago she got a letter from me requesting a donation for a Kittery Land Trust's purchase of nearby conservation land. She allowed it had taken her a while to figure out where I lived.

"I'm here for something small…but it could be big."

She let that enigmatic statement hang in the air a moment, while my mind grappled with what she meant. I knew where she lived, but nothing else about her.

I had met some of her family years before when soliciting for another KLT campaign. Glancing in the backseat of her car I saw a medium sized black dog

— a 'Service' animal with identifying collar and cape — lying in a cage.

"Oh, that's my dog Maggie. I'm disabled by the effects of meningitis. I have no short term memory — which requires me to take pictures of everything, and which limits me to doing just 2 things a day. Coming here is one of my activities for this Sunday. Maggie helps me get around. I couldn't do it without her."

Now I began thinking: this is a bit kooky. Her symptoms are strange, but her speech is coherent and appropriate. She has no obvious physical problems. The old doc in me began searching my brain for a diagnosis. Nothing came to mind.

She then handed me a $200 check for the land trust's Brave Boat Headwater's Nature Preserve Project. She said it was all she could afford because her support came from several trust funds that make it difficult to withdraw her money.

The next day she returned to my home "to take pictures." I learned that years ago her parents, both of whom she "intensely dislikes," took her off with them to a religious cult enclave on Cape Cod. The families' resources became tied up in that religious community — hence her trust fund problems. It seems that experience also necessitated subsequent years of psychiatric therapy.

I told her I understood how hard life must be for her and that $200 was a terrific contribution. I was touched by the donation because it apparently was a stretch for her.

"Well, the $200 is the 'small part' I mentioned," she replied. She went on: her uncle George F., her father's brother, used to live in York. Now, nearly 90, he lived with his disabled wife in assisted living quarters in Scarborough, but he always said Brave Boat Harbor was his favorite place in Maine. Her father had forbidden her to call or talk to Uncle George, which broke her heart because he was more of a parent to her than her father. Then she advised me to call him: not only does he love the Brave Boat Harbor area, but everyone in the family says "George has more money than God."

Uncle George had been the most pleasant, generous and successful member of a large, dysfunctional family. He joined the CIA as a young man looking for adventure. While maintaining a home and family in Washington D.C., he served long postings in India and Eastern Europe. His lengthy CIA career abruptly ended when "he was exposed as a spy in London." Smart investments over the years, plus a family inheritance, provided his summer home in York, and helped buy the family cottage in Kittery, several boats, and a comfortable retirement.

"Oh my, your Uncle George is someone I should meet, Sister C. How can I do that?"

She gave me his address and phone number in Scarborough. She emphasized I needed to remind him of his fondness for Brave Boat Harbor and that Sister C recommended my call.

Suddenly, visions of sugar plums danced in my head. From the improbable start, her story had created in me a premonition —a dreamy notion of a big donation: *maybe $50,000*. But, after years of fund raising, I knew not to anticipate gifts. I also knew I needed a good plan to turn my reverie into reality.

I sent a letter sent to Uncle George, introducing him to me and to the location, features and beauty of the BBH Nature Preserve. I then waited a week before I called him.

Uncle George, despite his advanced age, answered in a firm, resonant baritone. He immediately recognized my name and was familiar with the materials I had sent.

I was quick to reinforce my new friendship with

Sister C, and my knowledge of his love of the Brave Boat Harbor region of seacoast Maine.

"Ah, she's a difficult kid, Sister C. That move to the cult on Cape Cod was where most of her troubles began." The cult made her a nun: hence the name Sister "C."

"Yes, but she's very fond of you and knows how much you love southern Maine."

He told me that he did live in York for some time and back then had generously supported the York and other land trusts. But that was all in the past. He said he never thought he'd live beyond 85, and now that he had, he needed to watch his finances closely. My dream of a huge contribution began to fade. I desperately needed a way to rekindle his interest. Then, he did it for me.

"Any way, tell me some details about the campaign. I'd like to know about the financials."

I proceeded to give him the usual spiel, ending with the fact that we had raised 90% of the funds needed to complete the project and that only $200,000 more was needed. For a moment, Uncle George was silent. Then... "Well, I think I might be able to do 50."

"Excuse me, are you thinking $50?"

"No... I mean $50,000."

I gasped; "That's way beyond my expectations." It really wasn't. It's the amount I had first imagined when Sister C first mentioned I should call him.

"I want it to be an anonymous gift. No visits... no public announcements."

A check from Schwab Financial Services arrived 7 days later.

It was a fundraising experience for the ages... and my fantasy delivered.

REFLECTIONS

COMING OF AGE

EARLY JULY, 1956. Sixteen years old, a few weeks past high school graduation, you were in Paris with 17 teenage friends and 2 young-adult chaperones. Imagine you in Europe! Your first time far away from home, this 'City of Light' the first stop on a 7 week group bike-and-train trip through France, Germany, Switzerland and Italy. The cost then: $800, including cruise ship there, and a flight back.

VIN ROUGE

Even the 6 day Atlantic crossing to Le Havre was a blast. The passengers were mostly high school and college students who created a blur of awkward flirting and fast-dancing to Dixie-land music. After docking, your group took a train straight to Paris, arriving famished at Gare de l'Est in early afternoon. Before hunting for a hotel, the entourage commandeered the station's restaurant for lunch. Your entre to French cuisine was 'steak-frites'. The meat was thin and tough, but the 'frites' were terrific. You got tipsy on several glasses of Vin Rouge, a dizzy euphoria, pleasant and uncomfortable at the same time.

Inhibited by French culture and muted by little knowledge of the language, your daily diet that entire first week was simple; croissant with hot chocolate for breakfast, jambon sandwich for lunch, and steak-frites for dinner. You had learned your lesson and decided to adhere to strict moderation with wine.

BIERE

It wasn't until weeks later in Lucerne, Switzerland that you were again seduced by alcohol. Overwhelmingly so. A German-style beer garden, huge steins of foamy beverage, and stand-up/sit-down Bavarian drinking songs were the culprits. It was a huge lesson on the virtue of abstinence. A severe hangover was compounded the next morning by a group visit to a Swiss-cheese factory where the aromas would have nauseated a teetotaler. You coped for a short time before the pervasive odors roiled your intestinal turmoil. It's a recollection as embarrassing as it was messy.

COGNAC

Back in Paris that first day, The Metropole Hotel accepted your rag-tag, tired and bewildered student group for a week's stay. On the Right Bank, near Place de la Bastille, the neighborhood was more commercial than residential, especially in the evening when Parisian hookers occupied most of the street corners. To our disappointment, they all looked to have been in the business far too long. Worn and tired instead of colorful (as in the movie, Irma la Douce). Anything but alluring.

The hotel was a narrow, inconspicuous establishment. A dark, unpolished bronze plaque next to its single, glass-door entrance apologized; "Metropole Hotel: 2 Stars." It was only 4 stories high but looked tall because of the adjacent, one-story, Parisian side-walk bars. The hotel had no real lobby, just a narrow entrance hall.

A recessed reception desk on the left faced a 2-person French elevator on the right, a claustrophobic 'platform lift' separated from the hallway by a black metal, accordion-door. Its top speed; about 1 foot/second.

The rooms were tiny, old and shabby. Most had a sink, but the only full bathroom on each level was separate and shared. Few in our adolescent group knew what the porcelain fixture on the floor in our rooms was —a commode with sink fixtures? The explanation was shocking! Who knew? We slept 2-3 to a room. With no space for backpacks or suitcases, all luggage went down a slender, barely navigable, stone stairway to a damp, cool cellar for storage.

A little Parisian man and his wife constituted the hotel's staff. Mostly you saw only him —a 50ish, stumpy, balding grump with a lip-dangling Galoise cigarette dropping ashes down his dirty T-shirt. The evening before your group was to depart Paris, a chaperone asked you to help Monsieur le Proprieteur haul everyone's luggage up to the entrance hall at 6 am the next morning.

The transfer was finished by 6:30 am. The hotel keeper using simple sign language invited you to breakfast at the bar next door. Naively you were anticipating the usual: hot chocolate and croissants. You gulped when breakfast was delivered: 2 flutes of Cognac! And, it was not top-shelf Hennessy. This was a working men's bar.

Extracting his ever-present Galoise stump, your new friend gestured the only acceptable method of imbibing; throw-your-head back and down-the-hatch. All of it... at once. You were hesitant, but earnest Midwestern boys do what they're told.

There was a second or two before 'the pain' hit. First in your throat and then your stomach. You gasped. You cringed. You gulped for air. Tears blurred your vision. The locals fixed on your reaction, so you tried pitifully to pass-off your dense grimace as a knowing smile. They shot back amused smiles. Your discomfort and their silence seemed interminable. After a minute your composure returned. You sat there quietly and humbly another 10-15 minutes, pretending to enjoy the French banter, laughter and gesticulations. You then excused yourself to escape back to the hotel.

Your breakfast survival was the talk of the day in your group, heading that day to the Loire Valley and beyond. You had passed a French adolescent initiation rite. You were now an honorary Frenchman of sorts. All in all, Paris had been a sobering experience.

CATCHER IN THE RYE AND ME

WHAT A STRAIGHT-ARROW I WAS in high school. I'm not kidding. In pink shirts and baggy army pants, I dressed like all the other guys. Crew-cut, straight-laced, studious. I had 3 younger siblings and 2 annoyingly Republican parents. My mother was a former nurse and my father a doctor — medical school was my destiny. I was such a mid-western square I cringe thinking about it. I really do.

I worried all the time about how I looked. Acne blooms plagued me. I spoke carefully; my childhood stutter could pop-up anytime. So did spontaneous bursts of four letter words. Teachers were always reminding me; "profanity's the sign of a small mind trying to express itself." That made me feel bad. Honestly, it did.

In school I was friendly with everyone. I was a high school class-officer a couple of years. But nights and weekends I avoided the pot-heads, the beer drinking jocks and the party kids. I hung instead with the 'squares' — they amused me, and the 'brains' — they intrigued me. I feared hurting the family name, my father being a well-known doctor and all. Everyone knew him. It was hard. I couldn't do *anything* even a little bit out of line.

'Jane M.' was my girlfriend throughout high school. Her father was a doctor too. She was intelligent and achieving. Our Senior year we both got awards for "model behavior and academic accomplishment." We graduated high school as chaste as can be. Really. We were so well behaved it kills me. And, we both became doctors. How conforming is that?

When I was a high school senior I read *The Catcher in the Rye*. It described a life I'd never imagined, an outlook completely different from mine. It really did. I didn't know anyone like Holden Caulfield. He killed me. I don't mean I became Holden. That couldn't happen, given the basic me. But my previous conforming behavior and Boy Scout attitude took a big hit. Striving to be a model kid lost its luster. Being contrarian — at least some of the time — became an attractive possibility.

For instance, Holden denied most of the bad stuff that happened to him. As the book begins, he's contemplating a return to his parents' NYC apartment having just been kicked out of Pency Prep, already his *third* private school. If at all concerned, he hides it in cynicism. For instance, Pency Prep's motto was: "Since 1898 we have been molding boys into splendid, clear-thinking young men." Holden's take was;

"*Strictly for the birds. They don't do any damn more molding at Pency than they do at any other school. And I didn't know anybody there that was splendid and clear-thinking and all. Maybe two guys. If that many. And they probably came to Pency that way.*"

He made me wonder why I took everything so seriously. It would have killed me to have flunked one course, forget having been thrown out of three schools. Maybe I could never be as laid-back as Holden, but I decided I needed to relax a bit; when stressed, find the irony, maybe crack a joke or two. At least now and then.

Still, Holden wasn't indifferent. He could be a quite sympathetic. He cared about people and what happened to them, especially his siblings. Beneath his wary exterior was a soft heart and a moral conscience. There really was. In the story, Holden's lecherous roommate at Pency, "Stradlater," is preparing for a first date with a girl (get this; named Jane) who Holden remembers from childhood. She had been a favorite playmate of his. His concern immediately surfaced;

"I was so damn worried... if you knew Stradlater, you'd have been worried too. I'd double-dated with that bastard a couple of times, and I know what I'm talking about. He was unscrupulous. He really was."

After the date, Holden confronts Stradlater;

"What 'd you do in Ed Banky's dam car?..... Did you...?"
"That's a professional secret, buddy" replied Stratlater.
The next part I don't remember so hot. I tried to sock him with all my might.
Only I missed. I didn't connect."

I'm not saying I acquired moral indignation from Holden Caulfield, but he probably reinforced some I already had. In another scene, Holden declined a prostitute who came to his NYC hotel room. Now, I would have done that too. Superior moral strength or plain fear of an all-consuming guilt afterward? I don't really know. Same result, either way.

Like Holden, I never believed religious faith was necessary for having ethical and moral ideals. I grew up in a community rife with fundamentalist churches. I was a believer early on. With my adolescent convictions waning, I was emboldened by Holden's contempt for institutional religion. Really, my eventual conversion to secularism was rooted in *The Catcher in the Rye*. Here's some of Holden's influence;

*"...I got undressed and got in bed. I felt like praying or

something, but I couldn't do it. In the first place, I'm sort of an atheist. I like Jesus and all, but I don't care much for most of the other stuff in the Bible. Take the Disciples, for instance. They annoy the hell out of me, if you want to know the truth... while He was alive all they did was keep letting him down."

"The thing Jesus really would've liked would be the guy who plays the kettle drums in the (Radio City Music Hall) orchestra. I watched that guy since I was about 8 years old. He's the best drummer I ever saw."

Now I played the tympanies in our high school orchestra. So this part really knocked me out.

Holden spends a lot of time in the book identifying the "phonies" in his life, which seems to include about everyone he knows. As he explained to his girlfriend Sally;

"You ought to go to a boy's school sometime. It's full of phonies, and all you do is study so that you can learn enough to be smart enough to be able to buy a goddamn Cadillac some day, and you have to keep making believe you give a dam if the football team loses, and all you do is talk about girls and liquor and sex all day, and everybody sticks together in these dirty little cliques. The guys on the basketball team stick together, the Catholics stick together, the goddam intellectuals... the guys that play bridge...even guys that belong to the goddam Book-of-the-Month Club stick together. If you try to have an intelligent..."

"Now listen," Sally said, "Lots of boys get more out of school than that."

Old Holden answers her, but his insight is clouded by his worsening depression;

"I agree," said Holden. "I don't get hardly anything out of anything. I'm in bad shape. I'm in lousy shape."

I never could match his bipolar symptoms and mental deterioration. I get down sometimes, but nothing like Holden, poor guy. He did make me realize, though, that having a low threshold for phonies and their behaviors was a valuable survival tool. Necessary, actually.

J.D. Salinger took the book's title from a Robert Burn's poem containing the line;

"If a body meet a body coming through the rye." The author chose to paraphrase it;

"If a body catch a body...", so in the text Holden explained;

"Anyway, I keep picturing all these kids playing some game in this big field of rye and all. Thousands of little kids and nobody's around — nobody big, I mean — except me.

And I'm standing on the edge of some crazy cliff — I mean if they're running and they don't look where they're running and they don't look where they're going I have to come out from somewhere and catch them. That's all I do all day. I'd just be the catcher in the rye and all. I know it's crazy, but that's the only thing I'd like to be. I know it's crazy."

Crazy? Fantasy? Aimless? Maybe all of those. But how about his independence — his style and artfulness? How different from me — always driven, ever practical. No kidding.

Curiously, I eventually ended up imitating Holden's dream. I became a *'catcher in the city'* — over 40 years in the Children's Hospitals of Boston and Philadelphia attending babies and kids who were sick and approaching "the edge of" death. As it turned out, that too "was the only thing I'd like to be." 'Another connection with Holden that just kills me.

POST SCRIPT: The book circled back into my life when I was a 26 year old, bachelor Medical Officer in the US Navy.

Olongapo, Philippines may be the most degenerate village on earth. It's a jungle-side gathering of dark little bars, by-the-hour hotels and worldly prostitutes smack against the US Navy's Subic Bay Port. When my ship visited there several times during the Viet Nam War in

1965, I devoted hours to treating and counseling dozens of sailors who acquired STDs cavorting in Olongapo. Many were beaten up there too, and a few murdered. It's a dangerous, hell-hole of a place.

I decided I should *briefly* see for myself, one hot, boring afternoon, what the town actually looked like. I was never going to risk an evening there. The bar I entered resembled a ramshackle, wooden 'saloon' from the old west. Midafternoon, the place was already packed with sailors in 'civies' and Filipinas in flimsy outfits. I was sitting alone at a small table, sipping a cold beer, when a surprisingly dainty, pretty 20-something bar-girl slid onto the chair next to me.

"Hello. My name is Consuelo" started a mundane conversation, mostly about the sweltering weather, what ship I was on and where I lived in the States. Impressed with her intelligent face and nearly flawless English, I was also intrigued.

"How is it your English is so good?"

" I read a lot of books".

" Really? What books have you read?

" Well, *The Catcher in the Rye* is my favorite!"

Wow. What a shock. We actually had something in common. We intensely discussed the book and Holden Caulfield for sometime before I felt compelled to return to the security of the Naval Base. She smiled, shook my hand and disappeared in the dim light. Ten minutes later I was safe, back on ship. Lying in my bunk that night, and many times since, I marvel at the improbability of that encounter.

PUBLIC HUMOR

SITTING IN A LITTLE HAIGHT ST. COFFEE SHOP one Saturday morning in San Francisco, I was sipping an espresso and watching the front-window, sidewalk scene — scruffy guys and pretty girls in vintage clothing dodging homeless hustlers and day-glow shirted druggies wearing white rats for hats. I was alone in that hole in the wall place except for a dark haired woman seated at the front window, absorbed in her latte and a book.

Abruptly the serenity was broken by the persistent blaring of a car-horn. A small black car was blocked behind a red, double-parked SUV. The confrontation was right in front of our shop and the honking droned on for minutes before the SUV relented and both cars moved on down the street.

Annoyed, I said out loud, "Well, I guess there are bullies even here in laid back Haight-Ashbury."

"Oh, that man honking couldn't be a bully; he's driving a Prius," quipped the latte sipping woman. I laughed out loud...what a great line, even though I suspected she was being serious, not funny.

The next day I was looking for a place to sit in a busy Peet's Coffee Shop on the Berkeley campus. I spied a seat at a sunny patio table where a pleasant, elderly couple were already sitting. They waved at me to bring my coffee to the empty chair. I thanked them effusively, sat down and quickly immersed myself in some memoir writing.

My tablemates were equally self-absorbed. From their tasteful, modest dress and their intelligent conversation about local politics and music, I suspected they were part of the UC faculty. No matter: they chatted quietly and I wrote intensely for a half-hour or so.

Suddenly, they smiled, stood up and prepared to leave. Always willing to be a bit inappropriate, I pretended surprise and blurted out, "Oh, 'something I said?" Not missing a beat, the old gentleman impishly grinned, "No, 'something you wrote!"

I wanted to give him a high-five for such a clever retort, but they we gone before I could say anything more.

One of the joys of traveling is collecting 'zingers' from people along the way.

A DIAGONAL MOMENT

I'M A CAREFUL MAN...a prudent fellow. 'Anything but impulsive. Early in life I decided it was easier avoiding trouble than getting out of it. This cautious, plan-ahead behavior is why a few moments in my early 20's are so surprising — even shocking — to me now.

The University of Michigan's main campus in Ann Arbor is picturesque. The center of the campus and the heart of college life is a large city block bordered by ivy-covered, columned libraries and teaching halls. An endearing feature of that block is 'the Diag,' a 20' wide, concrete walk extending 3-400 yards diagonally from the block's northeast to its southwest corner. A popular site for pep rallies, protest marches, theatrical pranks and other college fun, it begins at one end with an arch through the Engineering School Building and extends to open green lawns with giant shade trees at the other.

Students, professors, tourists and lay-abouts crowd the Diag daily. Student high-jinks — bonfires, foot races, impromptu musicales and loony "lectures" — fill the evenings. The Diag is a people place, a busy sidewalk, bicycles being the only wheeled conveyance allowed there.

Ann Arbor, 1960. On a cool, grey spring day we were finishing our morning in the Anatomy Building about 2 blocks from the Diag. It was noon, and my freshman medical school anatomy partners, 4 men in their 20's, were hurrying to pack away our cadaver after a morning-long dissection gone overtime. We had half an hour to get lunch back at our medical fraternity house before our next classes at University Hospital. We 5 squeezed into my VW Bug and headed down S. University Ave. toward the Nu Sigma Nu House 5-6 blocks away.

As I drove by the Engineering School Arch, the Diag seemed to beacon to me; "Take a short cut" it whispered. I think I entered a mild trance then — I could hear the conversation in the car but didn't feel at all connected to it, my passengers, or to the outside world. I briskly swung hard to the right, bumped up and over the curb, braked slightly as we passed under the Engineering arch, and headed confidently down the pedestrian packed Diag. My dumbfounded companions, initially shocked into uncharacteristic silence, began shouting "what the hell...?" In my fugue state their excited exclamations seemed far away, like faint echoes from a distant hill. With a grin on my face, my eyes fixed on the dismayed and scattering crowd in front of me. Only faintly concerned about any Campus Police lurking nearby, I proceeded at 10 mph down the middle of that pedestrian walkway. I drove right over the large bronze U of M medallion embedded in the Diag's mid-point, a revered marker students are taught to avoid stepping on. My mind was unusually calm and detached, quite serene actually.

I drove almost the entire length of the Diag. before angling off to take another, rather narrow, sidewalk one block to our Huron Ave. fraternity house. The "what the hell" calls had turned to "are you kidding me..?"

and "what got into you ..?" taunts. My trance suddenly ended. I could again clearly hear their amazed voices. I was a celebrity, a hero, during the few minutes we had for lunch — the members of that medical fraternity thoroughly enjoyed and admired irrational behavior. I too was astounded by what had transpired.

And then everything was forgotten. Except by me. Although I've had a lifetime aversion to impulsive acts, I admit to truly relishing that particularly rash decision. My kids have enjoyed my retelling of the story, largely because it showed them a hidden side of their otherwise reserved, predictable father. Even my wife Kristin said recently: "How did that happen? It's so unlike you — it's so mysterious!"

UNCOMFORTABLE WITH UNCERTAINTY

As a 4-year-old shopping with my mother, I recall the slippery softness of her long fur coat under the stroking of my small hand. In department stores and other strange places that coat was my security, a source of reassurance. I also remember occasionally stroking by mistake the coat of a complete stranger, amusing to the involved adult but mortifying for me.

When 5, I cried as I waved goodbye to my Army Captain father as he boarded a troop train headed for France in WWII. My mother's insistent assurance of "he'll come back" prompted an emphatic "maybe not" from me, showing that pessimism does not require so many years to develop. Parents can underestimate how fully children understand the gravity of serious events. Parental denial is a useful tool. I often used it with my own children, and I find myself nostalgic for denial when required to explain difficult things to my granddaughter Ella.

A preoccupation arising in my mid-childhood was a fear of eventually having children of my own. I came to dread the thought of being a parent, even though my own parents were loving and supportive. It was what I saw around me that was frightening. Much of my childhood was spent in a large public park near our home, and my trips there usually started with this parental reminder; "don't talk to strange adults — there are people out there who steal and hurt children." Occasionally police came to the park looking for lost and missing children, suspected perverts and rowdy teenagers. The burden of parenthood seemed so overwhelming that by adolescence I had pretty much pledged myself to adult childlessness. Like politicians' pledges, my resolve turned out to be unsubstantial.

A result of my childhood insecurities, fears and anxieties has been controlling behavior worthy of the term 'character defect'. Even 'compulsion' or 'addiction' would not be overstatement.

When I, or someone close to me, has a problem my compulsive instinct has been to jump in and 'fix' it, the sooner the better. I know now my actions usually have been ineffective or made matters worse. I try now to remind myself when my anxiety rises that "it is not the end of the story": that things work out best when I offer sympathy and support, not solutions.

I have come to understand that my need to control is based in fear. I'm uncomfortable with uncertainty, whether the problem is personal, financial, marital, family — most anything. I try to manipulate people, places and events toward safe and secure outcomes. I jump in when one of my adult children is short of funds or in need of a job; my fearfulnesss causes me to rationalize giving or loaning them money, or using my connections to find them employment. Even if my fix eases my discomfort, it can be detrimental in the long run. Young adults need the confidence that comes from solving their own problems.

I know that my attempts to control the uncontrollable

are a delusion. Yet, in weak moments and without thinking, I easily head down a dark, familiar stairway where the steps bear the same sequential labels: anxiety > fear > worry > control. It's a habit I try to avoid, here in my autumnal years.

PERUSING THE NEWSPAPER

WE ALL FIND OUR AMUSEMENTS WHERE WE CAN. I like peeking in the nooks and crannies of the daily newspaper, where lurk vignettes of life's counter-currents and human foibles. Where else can you find material like this:

> *Police Log (Portsmouth Herald) August 2011:*
> *2:19 am – A Pine Street resident asked police to remove a woman from his home who "won't shut up."*

Or this in the same newspaper the day before:

> *Police Log August, 2011:*
> *10am: A woman told police she thought someone drugged her drink the night before. Sgt. Kuffer Kaltenborn said the woman reported having numerous drinks during the evening in question and police do not believe the public is in danger.*

Who knew Portsmouth police could be so dead-pan?
That same issue of the Portsmouth Herald was a veritable gold mine of fun stuff.

> *Police Log (August, 2011):*
> *8:04pm: Responded to the Route 1 By-Pass where a raccoon was struck and killed by a car and the driver was "attempting to bring it back to life."*

Yipes! I think I know that person. She's a Gerrish Island friend and an 'animal nut.' One evening several years ago she drove up my driveway requesting that I help her resuscitate a nearly dead fox in the street in front of our house. I demurred and she has been cool toward me ever since.

If anyone should ask I will deny it, but I'm also an inveterate reader of Personal Columns and Lonely Heart ads. On those pages the rubber of life meets the hard road of reality. Like this one from an English newspaper:

> *"Blah, blah, whatever. Indifferent woman. Go ahead and write. Box No. 3253. Like I care."*

Such resignation is common. So is brutally honest self-deprecation, as in this sample:

> *"Your buying me dinner doesn't mean I'll have sex with you. I probably will have sex with you though."*

Writing like that can come only from someone who is secure and confident — or perhaps confused and self-doubting.

The intensity of some authors shines through their submitted pieces, like the woman who wrote she was able to...

> *"start fires with the power of her premenstrual tension"*

While frankness is common in English self

advertisements, it's hard to imagine the attractive power in such a statement.

I like it best when journalists combine humor with profound wisdom, as did Sam Allis in the Boston Globe some time ago. His Sunday column about on-line dating contained this gem:

> *"I gave up long ago trying to figure what makes couples tick, but I will tell you the key to a 50-year marriage: a seamless neurotic fit. A seamless neurotic fit can be anything — he can wear heels and (she) can dress like a postman, he can breed guppies and she pit bulls. All that matters is that two pathologies occupy the same sympathetic angles of repose."*

The anticipated demise of our daily newspapers, and newsprint in general, makes me sad. Where will the nitty-gritty of life, described in memorable, humorous prose, come from in the future? Another problem: the content in E-print newspapers is confined and specific… no wide, 6-columned pages to casually peruse. For me that's too bad.

COMPULSIVE

I'M COMPULSIVE. It's not something to be proud of. Kristin says she didn't even know what 'compulsive' was until she married me. I am fairly functional, falling short of an OCD diagnosis (I think). But even without a psychiatric diagnosis, I still can strain our family's equanimity.

I prefer order. Actually, I need it. Before sitting down to write I tidy my desktop, and before starting a painting I clean up my studio. I can't just wash the car, I have to sweep the garage too. My focus on tasks is intense and I always finish what I start. I follow rules and guidelines carefully. It's effective to be compulsive, but not exactly fun. My threshold for frustration is pretty low.

My physician father once told me that what defines a superior doctor is "attention to detail." Naturally that advice was right down my alley and it paid dividends many times during my medical career.

An early instance occurred when I was just a medical student in Ann Arbor. I was assigned to a Medical Service whose patients were mostly pampered Detroit auto executives admitted for 'annual check-ups'. They were overwhelmingly in good health and anxious to pay well for several days of U. of Michigan Medical

Center attention. In fact they received rather perfunctory examinations from the medical staff because the chance of finding actual disease was small.

I, of course, approached the executive patients compulsively. One of the first was a rotund, stern-faced, but agreeable Chevrolet Vice-President without any complaints except that I was the 4th or 5th 'doctor' to examine him that day. Thorough as usual, I noticed something the professors and residents had not — an enlarged left tonsil. Subsequent biopsy revealed a localized lymphoma, a serious but very treatable cancer. Several weeks after successful radiation therapy, and overcome with gratitude, he mailed me 2 tickets to a Detroit Tigers' baseball game. I learned then that compulsion pays, but not all that well.

Just several months later I was an unconfident, beginning intern at the U. of Oregon Hospitals in Portland, Oregon. Working alone on a Pediatric Service on a July afternoon, I admitted an 8 year old girl whose behavioral problems had worsened after she suddenly had gone blind. A number of referring physicians, including eye specialists, had been unable to find the source of her blindness, complaining that her combative behavior prevented any thorough examination.

She was very resistant to my physical examination that hot day —crying and screaming, arms and legs flailing, head twisting difficult. After a sweaty hour or so trying to see her retina with my ophthalmoscope, my persistence paid off; tumor tissue in both eyes obscured all normal anatomy. No wonder the referring physicians had written in her chart "retinas not well seen." Although that stunning diagnosis considerably enhanced my reputation, it had nothing to do with medical brilliance. It was just compulsive habit: a refusal to give up just because the poor girl was uncooperative. [*The tumors were malignant retinoblastomas; her eyes had to be removed, but she survived]*

Those of us who are compulsive, perfectionists and workaholics are a pain to live and work with. We drive other people nuts, making complicated plans and fussing over details. I am notorious in my family, for instance, for nitpicking others about the way the dishes are done and the kitchen tidied after dinner: few meet my standards of thoroughness. My comments usually are more retractable than productive.

I tend to extend my own high expectations to others, and when those (unexpressed) expectations are unfulfilled, I resent it. Those resentments then become a problem, because the only way to relieve them is with forgiveness, itself a difficult process. It's hard to describe my compulsiveness as anything other than a character defect. Like many of my character defects, it's actually an asset taken to extreme.

Society and I seem to be conflicted on this subject. I have observed that nearly everyone privately wants a perfectionist carpenter, a workaholic auto-mechanic, or a compulsive doctor. They just don't want someone who's compulsive for a spouse, father, best friend or professional colleague: it's not good for their general, long-term serenity.

DAYDREAMING

GIVEN TIME TO DAYDREAM, a quiet room and the right mood, I can recall many vignettes and anecdotes from my youth — often fuzzy, but emotive, pictures of certain times, places and things. A sampling would include:

My first full sized bicycle — a red, Schwinn, racing bike with a narrow black seat, curiously curved handlebars and skinny wheels. 'Bought it myself for $60 with money saved from a paper route when I was 11, and then used it to deliver the papers, expand my world, and enhance my self-image. It was a marker, looking back, between boyhood and adolescence. I had several other recreational vehicles in my youth — motor boats, sleds, and go-karts, but my memories of them are vague and unemotional. They were diversions bought by my father. I alone invested in that red Schwinn.

Summers on Whitefish Lake — our cottage there, 30 miles from Grand Rapids, was the family summer home. Fun activities abounded — like water skiing, midnight fishing for bass or catfish, tennis with my Dad and brothers, grilled steak and cherry pie family dinners, and occasional car trips north through the "Vacation Land" that is Michigan.

Some favorite recollections revolve around the gang of kids who were neighbors throughout those hot, lakeside midwestern summers. There were 10-12 of us who grew up together, beginning as kids swimming from a home-made raft with a 5 foot "high dive", catching big snapping turtles and small animals, and competing in marathon games of Monopoly on rainy days. In adolescence, there were group rides on gravel country roads in Tommy McConnel's Model T coupe, garage dances, evening visits to the annual Sand Lake County Fair to loose money on "games of skill" and, if I was lucky, to hold hands with Bonnie while riding the Ferris wheel. When we were 13 and I was walking Bonnie home along the edge of the lake one evening, I 'stole' my first kiss (in truth, considerable planning went into it and required a lot of courage to carry out). One of her 5 sisters told me years later, it was Bonnie's first kiss too. I wonder if she shared my elation with that 'coming of age' moment.

Other adolescent memories abound. At 15, I was hired by my father to paint the exterior of our cottage, a one story, white clapboard structure of considerable girth.

I was instructed by my tradesman Grandfather on how professional painting was done, and my work was then inspected weekly by my perfectionist father. I earned $600 for the job and was proud to be told, when finished, that indeed, it was a "professional job." Looking back, I'm not sure whether I became a perfectionist that summer, or I already was one.

That was the same summer I first experienced grief when I discovered my boyhood Doberman, Lady, dead of old age under a backyard tree. I had to announce the sad news to the rest of the family, and then bury her in the woods behind the cottage. To compound my sadness, about the same time I lost a litter of baby squirrels I had been nursing for weeks. To my shame and horror, I put their cage in a sunny spot to warm them, got distracted for a couple hours, and returned to find them dead from the heat. I still feel guilty just recalling it.

About the only other regrettable memory I have of those Whitefish Lake cottage days occurred when I was about 18. It was a summer partly through my pre-med school years in Ann Arbor — a time when I was trying to assert my male independence, but conflicted by my dependence on my parents for college tuition, room and board and general well being. Relaxing on the cottage screened front porch one Sunday morning, my father and I managed to turn a pleasant conversation about my personal plans into a heated argument — as I recall, following his assertion that I was ungrateful for all he provided. I countered that, although I did appreciate his generosity, I didn't feel it gave him the right to tell me what I could do with my private time, and that perhaps I'd be better off not coming home so often. The next few moments are still pretty blurry — all I remember is his jumping up from his chair, turning as he stepped toward where I was standing, and throwing a haymaker right that I partially blocked and ducked. My mother shrieked while a guest neighbor woman gasped in fright. Then it was over. Everyone was breathing hard as I backed off the porch into the cottage. My mind has blanked out the hours afterward. There were eventual apologies and no long-term effects or hard feelings. I always think of it as another 'coming of age' event, but not one every young man should experience. With this exception, my dad and I had a really good relationship.

Thereafter, I spent 2 college summers as a camp counselor and waterfront director at YMCA 'Camp Manitoulin' near Grand Rapids. I was successful teaching boys how to row, paddle, sail and swim. Away from the waterfront, my successes were fewer. I hated taking the 10 boys in my cabin on overnight hiking trips, as was required of me every 2 weeks. I never could get a night's sleep in a hammock, and once (along with some other counselors) was caught by the Camp Director having a few beers "to promote sleepiness." I'm also embarrassed by a story my mother heard from one of my camper's parents. Her son related that to gain order and compliance from the kids in my cabin, I told them; "You know guys, I'm earning money here for medical school. If you are rowdy, talking loudly and fooling around after taps, I'll get fired. And then I'll never become a doctor." Now that's embarrassing — and deceitful: my parents furnished my educational costs. All of them.

In contrast to YMCA camp, my first 2 summers in medical school were spent indoors doing colorless, uneventful work. I was employed by my father as a darkroom technician in his large, busy radiology office. I spent whole summer days, except for a 1 hour lunch, imprisoned in a 4 x 8 foot darkroom, where in the glow of red 'safety' lights I daily unloaded and refilled hundreds or heavy x-ray cassettes, snapping the exposed film on metal holders to be immersed in successive tanks of developer, fixer and then clear water, before being placed in a drier. Nothing was automatic then: every film had to be developed by sight-inspection and judged for acceptability by me, who (as the bosses' son) was the target of considerable critical evaluation from the staff x-ray technicians. I spent a lot of time there in the dark, daydreaming of past bright days and good times at Whitefish Lake and Camp Manitoulin.

QUIET CAR

EARLY ONE DAMP, COLD MARCH MORNING in Boston I search along a bustling S. Station platform, looking for the 'Quiet Car' on the outbound 6:30 Amtrak train to NYC. There are as many incessantly ringing cellphones and inane, loud phone conversations among the Big Apple bound passengers as there are folded NY Times papers and expensive leather briefcases. Theoretically the Quiet Car will be my refuge from those diabolical cellular devices.

The Quiet Car is in the middle of the train. I grab a window seat just as the train pulls out. Snow dusted trees and track-side rubbish begin to blur as the stillness of the coach induces drowsiness quickly slipping into a short nap.

My reverie is short lived. Within minutes I'm aroused by a repetitive, quasi-musical cellphone ringer followed by a rather loud conversation coming from the young woman seated in front of me. Her cellphone is pressed to the side of her head. Instantly this is a problem for me, a self-confessed fairness-freak. I have a longstanding, largely unfulfilled, expectation that people talking on cellphones will be considerate and speak quietly. A brief debate breaks out in my head over whether to say something. Predictably, irritation trumps acceptance, and the self-righteous 'policeman' in me moves to action.

Leaning forward, in a condescending tone (a persona my wife calls my "white-knuckle Mr. Roger's act"), I politely remind the young woman that cellphone use is prohibited in the Quiet Car. Immediately, her well coiffured head spins around and I'm confronted by a teary-eye 25 year old, explaining (the phone at half-mast) that her conversation is crucial; "I'm checking on my baby who spent part of the previous night in an Emergency Room." Her presence on the train this morning, along with the laptop computer and business papers arrayed around her, suggested to me that the 'crisis' was neither serious nor sustained. I decided to say no more.

But I now have another dilemma; is my indignation more justified than hers? A cool resolution follows: I mumble something audible to her about "confused priorities," and she stomps off to finish the already lengthy call in the dining car.

Disrupted by feelings of guilt, resumption of my nap is futile. In the movies there could be a replay of the encounter in one of those 'alternative reality' settings which could go something like this: I enter the Quiet Car and take a seat next to a young business woman preparing for her day in NYC. After an interlude, we strike up a conversation and she mentions the troubling previous evening that found her in a local ER with her baby. I listen attentively and praise her mothering skills. We arrive in NYC, she departs for her day of business, and I head off to some art museums and galleries, both of us serene.

My overgrown sense of fair play, like many other traits, is both a strength and a character defect. It's most beneficial when I direct it at my own behavior. When I try to influence others, the outcome is invariably poor. The objects of my criticism usually are indifferent or hostile, proceeding to do whatever it was they intended. And I end up loosing equanimity.

In Al-Anon, they put it this way; "let it go or be dragged."

JOURNEY

"the opposite of faith is not doubt, it's certainty"
Anne Lamott

My dear granddaughter Ella, then 5, threw out this question from the backseat:
   "Grandpa, I believe in God but my mother doesn't!"
   "Well, some people believe in God, some don't. He's a mystery."
   "Grandpa, God is a She! I believe in God and I know she's a girl."
   "Ah, Ella, what do you want for lunch, sweetheart?"
   It worked. No more God-questions. Good thing. I've been an atheist for some years and didn't relish defending myself to a kindergartener.

My parents never talked about religion, never showed a preference or even interest. Toward the end of her life, my mother began attending church, but wouldn't discuss her motivation, obvious as it seemed. I'd like my kids to know what I was thinking.
   I could describe myself now as a 'Christian atheist'. I have rejected any conventional idea of God. Still, I adhere to most Christian ideals because I've lived a

lifetime in a Christian family and culture. But I am an atheist — or secularist, the gentler, contemporary term often used today. But it all began quite differently...

I am 7 years old. Again, at 9am on a Sunday morning, it's time for me to walk several blocks to East Congregational Church (in churchy Grand Rapids, MI) for the early morning service. As always, I go alone. My parents are puzzled, my siblings indifferent. Adult church members are impressed and encouraging, especially as I help distribute the collection plates, attracting prized "atta-boys" for my efforts. Despite being tone-deaf I'm also in the Children's Choir. It needs members and I show up consistently. I love the knee-length red robes with gold trim and the congregation's applause for our weak, but brave, efforts. For me, God is the bearded guy from Nazareth I hear about in Sunday school. I pray to Him occasionally; "Help me, help me, help me." [According to A. Lamott, the only other real prayer is; "Thank you, thank you, thank you"]

In adolescence I continue my faithful Sunday morning attendance, progressing to the Youth Choir, handsome in a black robe and white tunic. However, the Sunday evening 'Youth Fellowship' gathering really sparks my teenage interest. There are lots of girls there and only a few boys. It's the hormonal phase of my spiritual journey.

In college and medical school my church going diminishes, along with my interest in religion. Conventionally, I discuss God and related ideas in occasional study-break sessions. Following a pre-med philosophy course, I adopt pragmatist William James' view; "it is better to believe than not to believe." That keeps me in the fold a bit longer.

I muddle through midlife — academic medical career, marriage, family, retirement at 62 — progressively losing belief in a Supreme Being. My training to think scientifically contributes to the transformation. So does the influence of my wife Kristin, a lifelong atheist. Nearing retirement I attend (alone; again) the First UU Church of Philadelphia, more out of habit than conviction. Eventually that too ceases. I've become the lowest sort of Protestant: a lapsed Unitarian.

My atheism further evolved in retirement from two interests: one, a late-life attraction to westernized Buddhism and the other, a lengthy participation in Al-Anon. Both have similar philosophies—with one large difference: Buddhism requires no Supreme Being while Al-Anon's 12 steps are based on the need for finding a personal "Higher Power." Unlike most Al-Anon members, instead of finding my Higher Power, my '12-stepping' took me from 'weak follower' to 'nonbeliever.' As a result, now I'm less a 'Christian atheist' than I am a 'Buddhist secularist.' Christianity is a religion (it has rules for living), Buddhism is a culture (it's a way to live): Christians believe, Buddhists do not.

The central problem is not my ability to conceptualize God, but whether God in any form could have any idea of me. I just can't imagine that. What I do imagine is a positive force for compassion and kindness, an innate, gravity-like power beyond the God of religion, a vitality I can dial into for my own good or ignore at my peril. The choice is mine. That force can guide my intentions, but it doesn't care, help, reward or punish. For me, tuning into that ideal is much like Annie Dillard's concept of getting to know the galaxies; "if you want to (connect with the cosmos), you have to find a very dark place, far from ambient light and set up there with a chair and telescope. But the stars are indifferent —they neither need you or care about you."

The vocal atheist Bertrand Russell was once asked what if he turned out to be wrong —what would he say at the Pearly Gates? He replied; "I would go up to Him and I would say: You didn't give us enough evidence."

My own bet: no such hypothetical conversation is in the cards. No God. No self. No hereafter. No problem.

SAYING GOODBYE

'Omnes vulnerant, ultima necat'
(All hours wound; the last kills)

YOU ARE A YOUNG STAFF RADIOLOGIST, early in your career, at Boston Children's Hospital. One wintery night at 3am, you, a nurse and an x-ray technician are in a catheterization lab, trying to save an 18 year old girl with chronic, severe lung disease (cystic fibrosis). Despite heavy sedation, she is periodically coughing cupsful of blood. Her face is pretty but thin, her arms spindly; having devoted so much energy to breathing every day, she had no calories left for growing normal soft tissues. Brownish dried blood matts her dark hair. The slightly acrid, heavy, musty smell of the fresh blood pooling on the sheets beneath her permeates the room. She is exsanguinating.

Your task is to insert a tiny catheter into the artery pulsing in her right groin, advance it using x-ray/ TV imaging to the aorta in her chest, and then find, one at time, the multiple, abnormal arteries supplying her diseased lungs. Once located, you will plug each pathological vessel with tiny pieces of plastic-sponge to stop the bleeding. This is a technique you have developed precisely for this hemorrhagic complication of cystic fibrosis. You feel some stress...you are alone in this. No one else in Boston's medical mecca, or anywhere else, has a better solution or an alternative treatment. The pressure doesn't distract you; it intensifies your concentration and will to succeed. Years of training in the making, it's what you've always wanted to do... where you wanted to be.

Her name is Marie L. It takes several hours, but eventually you succeed that night. And, on 2 more occasions for her over the next several years. As with the many CF patients you eventually treat, you aren't slowing the progression of their chronic disease. You are only saving them and their families a frightful, uncomfortable, messy death. For that they are grateful. But wary too: each of those children's families bravely agree to the procedure even though you warn them that *'bronchial artery embolization'* could result in spinal cord paralysis. Thirty years later you were able to say that dreaded complication never occurred, although the threat of its happening was always there.

By age 21, Marie's cystic fibrosis has decimated her lungs. Back then, most people with CF died as teenagers. It was before the era of lung transplantation and effective medical treatment. She is admitted to CH for the final time, not coughing up blood, but just too tired to breathe any more. She is dying. The family asks that you stop by for a farewell visit. You haven't ever received such a request. You are unprepared and unconfident...wondering if you are up to the task. As a kid at 2-week summer camps, you couldn't even say farewell to your counselor without tears. A lifetime of carefully avoiding 'goodbye scenes' has caught up to you.

You put on a clean white coat over blue scrubs and plod up several flights of stairs to Division 36, a ward for medical patients. Passed a nursing station and down a long corridor, her private room was the last door on the right. With some hesitation you knock softly, then push the door open. About 10 adult family members and friends fall silent as you enter; faint, slightly embarrassed smiles and nods spread among them. They unevenly encircled a hospital bed on which Marie rests, propped up on pillows, eyes shut. She looks pretty as ever — her clean, black hair glistens and a slight bit of make-up hides her paleness and highlights her large eyes. A flowered bed-jacket modestly covers a violet nightgown. She resembles a book cover illustration for 'Sleeping Beauty."

Saying nothing, you nudge slowly through the gathering to the bedside at her left. Marie's breathing is slow, shallow and unlabored — gifts from a morphine drip. She isn't speaking, moving her limbs or opening her eyes. Death is usually more a process than a precise event. She is alive but barely. Possibly able to hear and feel, but unable to respond.

There is an aura of serenity in that hospital room arising from the inevitability of her terminal condition. No sense of emotional turmoil. Choking up, tearing and turning away are your usual ways of coping with farewells. If many there were wringing their hands and crying, your emotions would escape your control. In the quiet, reverent, "time to let go" peacefulness at her bedside, you are able to project sincere, dry-eyed compassion. Doctors are trained...admonished...not to cry 'on duty.'

Silent since entering, you decide to remain so except to whisper to the assembled group; "I'm Dr. Fellows." Moving closer to the bed, you grasp her left hand in yours, and with your right hand instinctively lean over to stroke her forehead, gently brushing strands of hair back to the top of her head. Your own physician father had large, soft hands. When you were sick in childhood, he often performed that same stroking maneuver. You never forgot how comforting it was. For Marie, you hope your own hands convey empathy and caring, well beyond any words you might utter. After a minute or so you straighten up, pat her forearm, nod to her parents and leave, conscious of a mute, dignified calm in the room.

If asked which is harder, trying to save a child's life or saying good-bye to a dying patient and family, I would affirm the latter. I discipline myself to handle emergencies unemotionally. Goodbyes I have to improvise: they are always burdensome, awkward and defeating.

ADDENDUM;

PRINCIPLES OF A GOOD DEATH*

To know when death is coming, and to understand what can be expected

To be able to retain control of what happens

To be afforded dignity and privacy

To have control over pain relief and other symptom control

To have choice and control over where death occurs (at home or elsewhere)

To have access to information and expertise of whatever kind is necessary

To have access to any spiritual or emotional support required

To have control over who is present and who shares the end

To be able to issue advance directives that ensure wishes are respected

To have time to say goodbye, and control over other aspects of timing

To be able to leave when it is time to go, and not to have life prolonged pointlessly

*Smith,R. 'A Good Death', British Medical Journal, vol. 320, #7728, 2000, pp.129-30

Another view: It's better to concentrate on living a good life than worry about having a good death.

DIMINISHED FACULTY

FOR NEARLY 40 YEARS, I was an academic physician taking care of patients and doing clinical research. In my retirement I recall caring for patients as important, rewarding, and satisfying work. But of all the clinical research I did, the papers I wrote and talks I gave, most is already dated and lacking any major long term impact.

Few were more specialized than I was; a Pediatric Cardiovascular Radiologist, a destiny part providential, part intentional. Born a 'congenital radiologist' (in my father's footsteps), my other interest became Pediatrics in med school. My career began at the Harvard Medical School and Children's Hospital, Boston in 1971 when a push to revolutionize the treatment of children with congenital heart disease was just beginning. Like a writer searching for a topic to encompass, I chose (pioneered) a new medical speciality, *Pediatric Cardiovascular Radiology*, because if was fascinating and ripe for clinical and academic research

My collaboration with Pediatric Cardiologists began when only primitive imaging techniques existed for visualizing complicated, abnormal heart anatomy.

We worked in cardiac catheterization labs on often deathly ill, sedated or anesthetized babies and children, struggling with cumbersome monitoring equipment and bulky imaging devices. We greatly needed major advances in our technology.

About 1975 a renaissance in cardiac diagnosis began. New electronic enhancement of x-ray images magically created clearer viewing of the beating heart. When it was combined with the intravascular injection of visible dye, accompanied by cine filming of the images, suddenly we saw in detail the complicated pathology of congenital heart disease. We learned to enhance this imaging by employing variable angles of view and by simultaneously filming from 2 directions. With so much information, instantaneous 3-D display of the pathology became possible.

Aided by those enhanced images, we began to use our catheters and other devices therapeutically— to close holes in the heart, open obstructed valves and vessels, and to plug sites of bleeding, all without incisions, stitches or other surgical necessities.

In the 1990s, the last decade of my career, new and advanced technologies appeared. Cardiac ultrasonography, computed tomography, and magnetic resonance imaging were revolutionary. Without requiring needles and catheters, these devices provided physiologic as well as 3-D anatomic information. Since my retirement in 2000, these innovative methods have largely replaced the x-ray imaging advances we thought were so advanced.

I have been left perplexed, fondly quoting Bennett Cerf's line; "Progress is fine, but in general it's gone on too long." I think this feeling results from my past faulty perspective. When active in the discipline, I was naïve enough to think I was running the anchor leg of a knowledge-relay race, and that we had "won" by learning so much and contributing so greatly to pediatric cardiovascular medicine. In fact, we were just part of a continuum, running a middle leg in a race whose finish line was still distant. I was just a participant, not a winner. Looking back after many years in retirement, I feel like "diminished faculty", a punning description what I am now, a medical-academic relic.

However, I do take solace in a recent encounter with a poised young Pediatric Cardiologist in Boston. She purposefully sought me out in a crowd of hospital alumni, saying; "Hello, Dr. Fellows. I'm Dr. Liu, the new head of the Cardiac Cath labs at The Boston Children's Hospital. I've heard lots about you and I just want to say thank-you for all you did."

I've felt better ever since. Somewhat less "diminished."

OBITUARY

Don't cry because it's over, smile because it happened.
Dr. Seuss

KEN FELLOWS DIED _____. Don't fret; unlike you, he doesn't have to get up this morning...or have to floss ever again. His wife Kristin and adult children Maria, Hannah and Jesse once asked him to write an "auto-obituary." Compliant to family, he offered this.

Ken ('Kenny' to a select few) was the first of four children of Bernice, a surgical-nurse mother and Ken Sr., his radiologist father. Born in Grand Rapids, Michigan in 1938, he was raised there with 3 siblings in a loving, fairly functional middle class family of the 1940's and 50's.

An energetic, gregarious student and attention-seeking class cut-up, he once asked his 4th grade teacher, Mrs. Driver, to estimate his academic potential: "B+" was her guess and accurate prediction. He actually enjoyed adolescence and high school, graduating at 16. Awarded the final AOA spot in his 1963 U. of Michigan Medical School class, he was an MD at 22. He did postgraduate medical training in Portland Oregon, San Diego, Boston, Ann Arbor and finally Hamburg, Germany in pursuit of becoming a board certified

Radiologist in 1973.

Ken resisted considerable pressure to join his father in the private practice of radiology, opting instead for a career in academic pediatric radiology. He began as an Instructor in Radiology at the Harvard Medical School and a Staff Radiologist at the Children's Hospital, Boston where he served 18 years. In 1987, Ken was named Professor of Radiology at the Pennsylvania School of Medicine and Radiologist-in-Chief at the Children's Hospital of Philadelphia, positions he held until his retirement in 2000 at age 62.

The intellectually stimulating atmosphere of university medical centers fostered his satisfying career caring for many patients and expanding some clinical frontiers. Since the patients were often the sickest of the sick, his work was fulfilled by dramatic experiences and some lives saved. His other great academic reward: the very many medical students and young doctors he taught and trained, each of them providing a proud medical legacy.

Beside his routine clinical work and teaching, Ken helped originate a new subspeciality, "pediatric interventional radiology." He used modern medical imaging, tiny catheters and other devices to stop major bleeding, close holes in hearts, drain abscess and cysts and do other surgical-like procedures in babies and children. Because of those new life saving techniques, he was essentially "on-call" for 30 years. When his son Ian was asked if he intended to follow in his father's footsteps, he always replied; "no, I didn't get the responsibility gene."

Over his academic lifetime Ken published 140 scientific papers, books and abstracts, gave over 100 international lectures, and for a decade was co-editor of the <u>Journal of Cardiovascular and Interventional Radiology.</u> Of course, none of this mattered to his children. Whenever hurt, ill or in need of medical advice, they begged and pleaded; "Dad, couldn't I see a real doctor?"

Ken's family was the best part of his life and his greatest joy. As a young U.S. Navy doctor living in Laguna Beach, California, he met and married Kristin Thorsdale in 1966. She became his life-long partner and inspiration. Intellectually stimulating, encouraging, and creative, she also was a full-time mother of 4, an inspired homemaker, a gifted artist and a beloved grandmother. A minister friend once offered... "you two have had a good run together."

Their marriage was blessed first by the birth of son Ian and daughter Hannah, followed by the adoption of Jesse from Korea and Maria from Columbia. Through all the rewards and heartbreaks, raising those children to become loving, independent adults was life's most worthwhile endeavor. The unexpected death of Ian at age 37 was also the saddest, most the difficult family event. Intense grieving was eventually eased by Hannah's accurate prediction that Ian's death "would bring all of us even closer," and by the gift of granddaughter Ella's birth to Hannah and Mike Marchand 2 years later. For both Ken and Kristin, Ella was the sunrise following the darkness—a reason for hope, joy and fun again. Ken happily spent hours amusing her and being charmed by her. She became his inspiration to seek a mythical "Grandfather of the Year" award at some imaginary time in his life.

Ken's love of travel began at age 16: he hostel-hopped the summer of 1956 through France, Switzerland and Italy with 17 other teenage friends and 2 adult chaperones.

He discovered in those early travels he had an acute sense of direction. One early morning as the group was boarding a French train, Ken noticed it was headed in the wrong direction. Unable to convince even the adult leaders, he stepped back onto the station platform, waving as the group departed. Remaining there on the station's benches, he welcomed them back, smirking only slightly, several hours later.

That eye-opening summer travel ended his Midwestern provinciality. It was replaced by a quest to see as much of the world as possible, and to have as many foreign friends and memories as he could. His medical training on the West Coast and subsequent duty as a 25 year old Naval Medical Officer traveling the Pacific to the Philippines, Japan and Vietnam furthered those ambitions.

Working in urban American medical centers, Ken developed friendships with visiting doctors from around the world. Medical meetings and volunteer medical service took him, and often Kristin, to India, China, Poland, Australia, South America, South Asia and most of Europe. His family over the years enjoyed reciprocal visits with families in Germany, Switzerland, England, and Scandinavia. In retirement Kristin and he favored southern France for vacations, often sharing a rental residence with Swiss and American friends. On occasion Ken actually contemplated being reincarnated as a Frenchman, but was ultimately dissuaded by a young French doctor friend who warned; "Don't! They are far too complicated, you know."

Ken was a perpetual athletic "wanna-be". When only 5 or 6 he won a few citywide swimming contests. With only modest success he swam competitively in high school and college (where, to encourage him to swim faster, his teammates often knelt by the pool's edge shouting "sharks, sharks" during his races). High school baseball, recreational softball, pick-up basketball and pond ice hockey were other sources of exercise, fun and friends throughout his life. Luckily, he was still playing basketball and pond hockey well into his 70's. He always said that life could get no better than being out on a winter's day under a sunny blue sky, skating on smooth pond ice with sticks, pucks and a gang of good friends. He also fantasized that the best end to his life might come on a basketball court, where the last words he would hear are: "Nice shot."

Another lifelong interest of his was volunteer service. Whether organizing neighborhood ice-skating, coaching youth soccer, being president of national and international medical societies, serving on the boards of York (ME) Hospital and the Kittery Land Trust, or being appointed to Kittery town committees and commissions, he tried to contribute to organizations and communities. For him, volunteerism fulfilled the admonition "to always leave a campsite in better shape than you found it." And these activities kept him happily engaged in his later years, so much so that Kristin often remarked as he left for still another meeting; "I sure am glad I'm not you." He also found truth in this quote from Tagore:

I slept and dreamed that life was a joy. I awoke and found that life is service. Behold, service is joy.

Retirement to Kittery, ME at age 62 (he started early) allowed expression in a new part of his life, watercolor painting. In his later years he was happy painting and exhibiting landscapes of Kittery, Stonington and Monhegan Island, Maine. Also, he created portraits of his beloved Ella. Painting became his escape, his inspiration, and his contentment. Along with teaching watercolors, it also meant he was never bored— never without something he loved doing. His painting brought about a lifetime-transition: someone, in nearby Portsmouth, NH, when asked if she knew Dr. Ken Fellows, replied; "I don't know the doctor, but I know an artist, Ken Fellows."

He owed his enjoyment painting to the guidance of several gifted Maine artists: Dewitt Hardy, Norman

West, and David Dewey. He was also blessed by the severe, but accurate, criticism of his wife Kristin and daughter Hannah. In medicine, art and general living, Ken's life was sustained and enriched by a vast number of family members, friends and mentors to whom he sincerely needed to be, and sincerely was, grateful.

Another valuable diversion and interest in retirement was Ken's commitment to memoir writing for more than a decade. A string of 80 short legacy pieces formed a compilation of his life's experiences that was published for his progeny as "bits and pieces of a life's mosaic." Years of practice in a writing workshop taught by his friend Rebecca Webb made the effort enjoyable and passably readable.

Rather late in life Ken embraced many insightful ideas and experiences he absorbed in Al-Anon meetings. Buddhist philosophy and secular humanism also became guiding forces in his thinking. Although he always enjoyed the humor lurking in life, if he had it to do over there is one change he would make—to just lighten up. Less intensity would have been easier on him—and everyone else.

For solemnity flows out of men naturally, but laughter is a leap. It is easy to be heavy, hard to be light.
C.K. Chesterton

CHANGING

Sublimation. Modification of an instinctual
impulse to socially acceptable behavior.
[Latin *sublimare, to elevate*]

I CAN'T TRULY REMEMBER DOING IT. But I heard my mother so often describe my diabolical, early childhood quirk, it seems very real to me. Even now, late in life.

Between the ages of 3 and 5 it seems, I was a mini-scourge, a neighborhood predator. Rumor has it that on occasion I lay in-wait on our red-bricked front porch for a strolling mother pushing a baby carriage. Seizing the opportunity, I would dash off the porch and down our short, sloping front yard to the sidewalk. There, before the startled mother could react, I'd slap or poke the sleeping infant. However satisfying for me, these incidents led to fractious, embarrassing confrontations for my poor mother.

There is evidence that the root cause of my waywardness was sibling rivalry. I was an only child until my sister Marcia was born when I was 3. Before I began attacking strange babies I was infamous for propelling Marcia in her high-chair across the linoleum kitchen floor into a pantry-closet. My way of 'disappearing' her for a while, I suppose. No fleeting thing, my attitude improved in regretful slow motion until, as senior adults, we have finally reached a mature, caring sibling relationship.

A question lingers in all this: was my becoming a pediatric interventional radiologist a sublimation of my malevolent childhood misdemeanors? For 35 years I used high-tech imaging devices (x-ray-fluoroscopy, ultrasound, CT) to perform para-surgical procedures (to correct heart defects, stop bleeding, open obstructions) in children. In harshest light, I ended up sticking needles and catheters, albeit under local or general anesthesia, in babies and children. It's hard not to call that a sublimation of early, dark behavior, which was so bad, as Anne Lamott says, "it would make Jesus take a shot of gin from a cat's dish."

ANOTHER CHANGE

Transformation. A marked change in appearance or character, usually for the better. [Latin trans, beyond + forma, form]

Art is an interest where transformation, rather than sublimation, occurred for me. As a child and adolescent, art was not part of my life. I wasn't creative. In school, I had only quotidian drawing skills, a personal frustration because my 2 brothers were really good draftsmen and cartoonists. My parents had no interest in visual art, so I never went to museums except on boring school trips.

In my 20's I married Kristin, an artist, knowledgeable in art history since childhood. I began to learn what I had missed: we discussed art at home, visited museums on our travels, and collected modest 'works on paper' along the way. However informed and interested in art I became, I never had a notion of being creative myself. Kristin, on the other hand, continued making art in many forms—painting, silk-screening, crafting clay, paper and other materials—throughout our 50 year marriage.

I did a little drawing in my mid-adult years. Doctor's are required to make notes in patients' charts describing details of the procedures they have performed—what was done, where tubes and devices were placed, and what follow-up care is needed. I found these post-procedural notes where clearer when I made labeled, anatomic drawings of what I had done instead of word descriptions. Over 40 years, I made hundreds of those diagrams which nurses and other doctors liked and encouraged. But they were just penned, utilitarian sketches. Not art.

When I was 50 and contemplating retirement in my early 60's, I began looking for something to do after medicine. I had seen too many forlorn, old docs hanging around hospital corridors and conference rooms, bored because they hadn't given much thought to the late phase of their lives. Kristin suggested watercolor painting would suit my personality—a process involving drawing and painting that requires planning and detail. What she actually said was; "Watercolors are perfect for a compulsive guy like you."

I've been painting for over 25 years; 10 years of taking drawing and painting lessons, and many more years on my own painting and teaching watercolors. I try to paint at least 2 hours a day in my home studio where I produce about 10 finished paintings a year, enough to have 1-2 public showings annually. I sell some of my work, give some away to friends and charitable events, and save the rest for my kids and grandchildren. Producing those paintings is pure pleasure; the process of drawing and painting completely engrosses me. Hours pass without notice. I paint any subject that attracts me. I turn down most offers to paint for commissions because income from painting is not an object. For the same reason, I don't have a web-site or seek other commercial venues. What I do is fun: tainting it with 'business' would bring distractions that would make it something 'other.'

    I had no idea that my dabbling in watercolors would become more than a mere diversion in my retirement. It became a 'second act' in my life. I once mentioned to my favorite local artist and mentor, Dewitt Hardy; "I can't imagine my retirement without painting."

    "That may be, but it helps to be good at it," was his wry reply.

OBSTECTRIC'S INTERN:
36 on/12 off

I.

WHEN YOU DELIVER 132 BABIES IN 45 DAYS, the average is 3 per day — a lot for an intern planning to be a Radiologist. It happened to me in 1964 during my rotating internship in Portland, Oregon and it required a grueling '36 hours on/12 off' schedule throughout a 2 month obstetrical experience.

Upon completing that rotation, 2 other single interns and I stole a rare day skiing at (ironically) Mt. Bachelor, 2 hours south of Portland. We had blind dates — coeds from the U. of Oregon. My date, "Patty" I recall, was an attractive Junior who had once been Portland's "Rose City Festival's Queen." Lucky me.

After a good day on the mountain, the 6 of us headed for the slope-side Mt. Bachelor Lodge, a mammoth log-framed structure, for drinks. Nestled around a huge, warming, stone fireplace, we settled in a cushioned 'pit' with our beverages. The 3 couples separately engaged in conversation, each inaudible to the other above the crackle of the fire and a loud restaurant din. Patty and I were reviewing the day's events, when she abruptly asked what I did as an intern. "Oh, I have a monthly rotation," I said. "Every 30 days I'm on a different service — like surgery, or pediatrics or general medicine. The patients' care is mostly my responsibility, but I always have residents and senior attending doctors to advise me and, when necessary, bail me out."

She was surprised at the length and difficulty of what was expected of an intern.

I explained that it all seemed part of a process to make young doctors responsible, and to toughen them to long hours and intermittent stress. Most of that year I was on call and in the hospital every other night: the 2 months on Obstetrics which was even tougher: 36 on /12 off, I told her in a shameless ploy for sympathy.

When she asked me why I had 2 months on OB, I told her that I had accepted a trade and took an extra month thinking — maybe, just maybe — it would work out that I didn't need to sleep during the 12 hours off and could sneak away to Mt. Hood (near Portland) for a few hours of skiing. "Bad bet. Never happened," I related.

"You poor guy. All that work. And most of the time you're looking at females' private parts. How does a young man like you deal with that?"

Because the ambient clamor around was louder, I raised my voice a bit;

"There's a lot to worry about in the delivery room. Two lives are always at stake and risks lurk everywhere. There's no time and it's no place for sexual arousal. 'Just part of the training too: medical things go in one compartment, human, ordinary life considerations go in another."

Suddenly, the noise level faded precipitously, and in a moment of almost pure silence, she blurted;

"Oh, I get it. So you really need more sex than most!"

My friends, and another 20 or more couples, were within earshot. Heads spun in our direction, eyes wide and faces flashing in wry smiles and giggles. Patty and I smiled sheepishly in the subdued light of the bar while I suppressed a strong urge to explain.

That was the lightest event of my obstetrical training. Several other experiences were memorable, not humorous: they were variably serious, pathetic, or tragic.

II.

My entire 2-month OB experience was at Portland's Multnomah County Hospital, a public institution where most ('ward') patients didn't pay. Although an OB resident was "on call" to assist or give advice, after 3 weeks I was pretty much on my own to manage the labor, delivery and post-partum care of the ward patients. This was more independence than in the rest of my internship. In a delivery room things happen suddenly, which was another source of stress: often without time to get help, I had to handle complicated events myself. Age 24, just months out of medical school, I was not confident in deciding life defining decisions. Several experiences still haunt me.

One was the midnight delivery of an alcoholic American Indian woman admitted from Portland's skid row well along in her labor. Communication with the 40 year old, bruised, puffy faced woman was limited by her inebriation and halting English. We barely had time to prepare the delivery room when a weak, pale, very premature baby boy was delivered precipitously, barely alive. The immediate question was to resuscitate or not?

The supervising resident and attending neonatologist were not immediately available. As do most interns in a crisis, I asked the nurses what in the world to do. They advised this was not a time for heroics: this baby had slim chance of survival even with intensive care (it was 1964). So we kept the baby warm and comfortable. Worried and anxious for it to be over, I checked on the infant several times before he died an hour or two later. Many times since, I've questioned my justification for not doing more to preserve that baby's life. I'm still conflicted about it, more now than at the time it happened. My thinking back then was less nuanced than it is now. It takes more maturity than I had then to realize how precious life is and how to practice compassion fully. At least, it was a lesson in learning to live with the medical decisions I made.

On New Year's Day, 1964 I delivered the first baby born in Portland (at 1:26 am), a guaranteed media event. The 35 year old mother, calm and plain faced, already had 5 children. Her sleepy affect and vacant stare suggested borderline intelligence. On rounds later that January 1st morning she announced she had named the baby boy "Noah." Her nurse quietly reminded us that local TV cameras would be there soon to film the 'first in '64 celebrity mother and child' for an evening newscast. She suggested someone remain nearby when the mother was interviewed, "just in case."

It was good advice. When the woman reporter asked the mother how she was doing, as the cameras rolled she volunteered; "I've already named my baby. His name is…ah, we're going to call him…, ah….?" The head nurse jumped in, "His name is Noah. It's a great name." The mother brightened; "Yes, that's it. Noah." The reporter quickly directed all remaining questions to the nurses. Noah was a 'star' at a few hours of age, but his introduction to the public was awkward, his life off to a quirky start.

Darlene, a young, first time mother, arrived one morning having mild, infrequent contractions. She was slightly built with thin arms and legs and a pretty but glum face framed by disarrayed, blond hair. Behind pursed lips and teary eyes, she was withdrawn and fearful. For good reason. She was 15.

Distracted by all the medical information I needed to glean, and then by preparations for her delivery (large-bore IV, timing her contractions, determining the baby's lie and her degree of dilation, among others) I neglected to ask an important part of her history. It was a nurse who filled me in: the baby's father was her mother's 46 year old boyfriend. Suddenly her joyless, fearful behavior was understandable: far more than adolescent immaturity, her apprehension was complicated and overwhelming.

Darlene's labor was particularly prolonged, compounding her pain and depression and enhancing the turmoil of her caretakers. A spinal anesthetic eventually eased her discomfort and was followed by the routine delivery of a normal infant girl. Knowing she had decided to put the newborn up for adoption, and by previous agreement with the delivery room staff, the nurses whisked the infant away without comment and out of sight of the fatigued, groggy mother. Postpartum, a few minor complications occurred, but they contributed little to the pathetic sadness of her situation and what probably was an extended period of depression and maybe a lifetime of resentment and regret.

I grew up a lot delivering 132 babies back then. Obstetrics exposed a part of life quite foreign to me—raw lessons in life's complexities and realities. More than my other internship rotations, that OB experience swept away much of my young man's innocence about the myriad paths peoples' lives travel.

50 YEARS TOGETHER

FIFTY YEARS AGO, Kristin and I married in Laguna Beach. We were in love then and still are, but perhaps like your marriage, it wasn't a straight-line experience. Reality and other bumps along the way leave me in no position to offer marital device. Same thing about child raising: before we married I had several theories about child rearing: now, after 4 treasured children and 1 grand, grandchild— I have none. 'Things' work out— mostly.

We said 'I do' with the standard vows on July 2, 1966 —most of which we upheld, at least intermittently. The contemporary trend is to individualize those vows with phrases like "I will always be your best friend", and "I'll never let you down." I appreciate the intent, but... really?

Do they think there will be no fights about...who spent how much on what?...why are *your* relatives coming again?... who needs a new car more? I submit, at some time you may look at your spouse and feel rage— at other times you'll gaze at this person you once adored and think "sure would be nice to have this whole place to myself."

Susan Piver is a favorite authority on marriage; she

authored "The Hard Questions: 100 Essential Questions to Ask Before You Say I Do." This vignette sums up a lot:

The other day, we had a fight (my husband and me). It was bad. Super bad. Bad like leaving-the-house-at-one-in-the-morning-to-go-sleep-on-the-couch-in-my-office bad. I can't even remember what it was about…..well, maybe I can, but I just don't want to believe that something so unbelievably stupid (someone not telling someone else that they bought a new camera, for example; I mean it only cost $200 and I needed it for work) could cause two normally sane people to absolutely lose their minds and jump all up and down yelling at each other. I mean, for goodness sake.

I dragged my self home at 6 am, dreading seeing him, but also hoping I would so he could see that I was still ignoring him. As I let myself in and walked up the stairs to our bedroom, he was exiting the shower, towel around his waist. Although I was still angry, I could see that he no longer was. He came toward me and held his palms up to me like two "hold it right there" signs or, possibly, two "OK, OK, I give up" signs. My palms spontaneously rose to mirror his, whether to stop him from coming closer or to hold him to me, I couldn't tell. In that moment, I realized I was trapped. I couldn't push him away, nor could I hold him close enough. **I couldn't keep him at bay because our lives are no longer two separate-but-parallel tracks as they were when we began living together. No. We're living one life together now. I don't know how or when this happened.**

When we said our wedding vows years ago, what we entered is "an impenetrable arc of uncertainty" (Susan P. again) that will end only when we finally say goodbye.

Like you and many others, our 'one life together' has had plenty of highs and lows.

We're still here not just because we loved each other, but we were also committed to the union. Another writer, Judith Viorst put it this way:

The big advantage of marriage is that when you fall out of love with each other, it keeps you together long enough to fall in love again.

(July 2, 2016: Kittery Pt. 50th celebration)

THOUGHTS, CLIPPINGS AND SCRAPS

I spent 40 years as an academic physician in two Pediatric Centers: Boston Children's Hospital and The Children's Hospital of Philadelphia (CHOP). I experienced the satisfaction of dramatic, life saving successes, and was overwhelmed by occasional devastating failures and heart breaking deaths. Casual visitors to these Pediatric Hospitals often remarked that the suffering they saw --or projected – affected them severely. They frequently asked me "how do you stand it?" When it's your job... when you are engrossed in solving devastating problems and helping save lives...your focus is narrowed, concentrated on what can be done, not what might happen. The human misfortune of the kids and their families, while omnipresent, cannot distract from the problem at hand.

I've always struggled to describe what happens at the extremes of life in a children's hospital. Then I recently found the following memoir piece by a CHOP colleague, **Dr. Steve Ludwig***. A better description of the effects pediatric disease can have on a child, the parents and the pediatrician would be hard to find.*

COMPROMISE

HIS PARENTS' EYES FILLED WITH TEARS as they described their son Chris, all boy— mischievous, fun loving, exuberant, competitive and above all when cleaned up and tucked into his bed— loveable.

Now Chris was here, in his Children's Hospital bed, in the ICU. He was a stocky little guy, hair cut short, tanned from playing outdoors all spring.

School was about to close for the summer break and I flashed back to my own time— sitting on the back steps of my house, lacing up my sneakers and contemplating an entire summer stretched before me. A summer was an eternity— one endless game after the next.

Like Chris, I loved baseball. The end of school and the beginning of a summer of fun— that was the season of seasons!

They seemed to be a wonderful family. Chris was the third of three boys. The parents were fully dedicated to bringing them up right and not afraid to having abundant amounts of laughs along the way.

Chris, being the youngest of the trio, was allowed the most latitude. The older brothers thought he "got away with murder," which only stimulated them more to include him in any trouble they could contemplate.

We sat in a small conference room. I had explained to the family that we now knew what had made Chris weak, so weak that he could not even breathe on his own. It was an infection of the spinal cord that left him paralyzed from the chin down. His every breath was dependent on the ventilator that attached to his lungs through a tracheotomy that the surgeons had placed in his neck.

Unlike the often-temporary form of this weakness known a Guillain-Barre Syndrome, this type was transverse myelitis. It would be permanent. Forever.

The father broke down and wept. He produced those giant, sobbing tears that erupted from somewhere deep inside him. His massive shoulders heaved with a force that mirrored the tearing apart of his insides. He was far more than heart broken.

The mother comforted her husband in a way that I would have liked to— but after all, I was their son's physician, professional, and a relative stranger. She wrapped her arms around him in a tender way— got his heaving shoulders and sobs under control.

"John, remember, we prayed to God to spare his life. Our prayers were answered. Now we will deal with what we have. We will take him in the condition he is in and work with him." Her words struck a responsive cord and with the father. They had asked *only* for his life. They had made the first compromise.

I was impressed with the way they helped each other. There would be times later on when he was the one to comfort her pain.

As our conference went on, the subject that I had dreaded most came to the surface. Somehow, I knew it would and that was why the dread was there. Who would tell Chris? Without any debate or the casting of any formal ballots, the vote was clear— two against one— they wanted me to do it. This wasn't the way it was supposed to be. It was all about saving lives, smiling cooing babies, getting people well, shaking hands and thanking you, as they walked out of your office, happy, healed, healthy.

I considered delaying talking with Chris for a day or two. Procrastination had worked for me many times before. But that wasn't fair. Now that the parents knew, he should know.

Approaching the boy I did not know what to control first— the unswallowable lump in my throat, my rapid heart rate, or my own tears ebbing just beneath the surface. He had not yet learned to use the overflow air from his ventilated breaths to make speech sounds, but I was able to read his lips and his eyes.

I explained his condition to him as I had to his parents. I got to the word "permanent."

I could see him try to process the information.

His lips moved, "So I won't be able to run again?"

I answered him with a 'no'— the word seemed to weigh a ton.

Again, he looked for clarification. "I can't walk?

This time I could only shake my head from side to side, the words could not get around the lump.

It had been many years since completing my residency. This was the hardest day. It was a day that made you question. How could this happen to anyone: Why should it happen to Chris?

Still processing, I could see his eyes search for some of the same answers to the same questions that I had in my mind. He didn't cry. How could I?

Finally he asked, "Will I be able to leave the hospital? Can I go home? Can I go to a Phillies game? He too had made the compromise.

I've now been retired over 15 years, which means I read that story more as an ordinary father and grandfather than a physician. I'm now soft as a grape, and an anecdote like this buckles my knees, tears my eyes. At the same time it reminds me of what I often saw during my working days — parents with unfathomable love, stoicism and foresight, children with immense courage, flexibility and insight, and pediatricians with staunch compassion, loyalty and wisdom. It doesn't happen everyday in a Children's Hospital, but often enough to be both humbling and inspirational.

FADING MEMORIES

We forget all too soon the things we thought we could never forget. We forget what we whispered and what we dreamed. We forget who we were."
Joan Dideon

HONEST, EFFECTIVE MEMOIR WRITING depends on fairly accurate recall. Approaching my 80's, memory is a tricky resource: even ordinary conversation can be an adventure. It makes me empathetic with the child who observed, "Memory is the thing I forget with."

Here in my 'anecdotage,' I've had to develop compensatory measures. One ploy I gleaned from the obituary of an elderly aunt, who when queried about something past, consistently replied, "Well, how soon do you have to know?" I since have adopted this clever phrase to cover for my habitual inability to quickly recall names and other buried information.

Writer Roger Angel describes another handy tactic. He noted in his 90's that words and facts often failed him in conversation. To compensate, he offers; "When talking I send an Indian scout into the upcoming sentence, searching for missing words, names and phrases. Alerted, I can change the context or content to avert the impending void." To some extent, this very maneuver seems to arrive naturally with aging.

Familiar scenes from childhood are now foggy and confused. Some accumulated distortions showed up starkly on my recent return to the neighborhood of my youth in Grand Rapids, MI (1940 - 1956). Our red brick, 2-story bungalow at 1238 Alexander St. is still there, but much smaller and homelier than remembered. The 4 block walk I made on short legs to Alexander Elementary School I recall as long hikes, while my Sunday morning 4 block treks to East Congregational Church always seemed short. The winding, middle class streets of my Grand Rapids Herald paper route I remember as boulevards, and the houses grand with expansive front lawns. That's not true now, and never was.

It's always curious that recollection of my schoolmate's faces remains fixed –so when a name from my distant past arises, I think their face is as it was in our school yearbooks. My mind makes no adjustment for seniority. I still imagine that the body types, hairstyles and personal mannerisms I so clearly recall are unchanged too. This is more than memory distortion, it's delusion. As a result, attending my 50th high school reunion was uncomfortable because so many friends there were unrecognizable to me. Theirs' were not just faces grown unfamiliar, but people I no longer knew at all. Of course, some lives had been a mess, others successful. I couldn't tell from appearances –every one was dressed well, smiling and gregarious. I felt so strange and stressed in the company of those former friends. They echoed the midwestern provincialism I fled as a young man. Their conservatism seems pervasive and their lives centered mostly on the Florida retirement communities they flee to much of every year. I have nothing in common with them now – whereas 60 years ago our lives were intimately entwined. I didn't go to our 60th reunion. Enough with 'nostalgia.'

I don't have to travel to class reunions to see aging's effect on old friends and their memories. There's evidence close at hand. I've been meeting for a weekly coffee with several local tradesmen for nearly 40 years –at Rick's in York for years, but now Lil's in the Foreside. Over the past several years I've added another crone group of retired doctors meeting monthly for breakfast. The average age at both gatherings is 75. The mental deterioration, individually and collectively, is distressing. Adding in the present deafness of some of the attendees, both meetings can become humorous skits on how old men end up bellowing, blustering and bantering-over each other while expounding the same stories, anecdotes and jokes they told at the last meeting. When a 'young' (60-70) retiree seeks to join one of these gatherings, I try to dissuade them. What I find as natural and mildly humorous regression of the old, newcomers may find depressing, even pathetic.

There's an apocryphal joke that illustrates our plight:

> *Scene: 2 old men in living room.*
> *Codger 1:* "We had a great meal at a restaurant last night."
> *Crone 2:* "What's the name of the restaurant?"
> *Codger 1:* " I can't remember, but help me here. What's the name of that popular, red flower everyone sends on Valentine's Day?"
> *Crone 2:* " A rose?"
> *Codger 1:* "Yes, that's it." *Shouting into the kitchen:* "Hey Rose, what's the name of the restaurant we liked last evening?"

And so it goes.

POST TRUMP ELECTION: A LETTER TO MY CHILDREN

Nov. 9, 2016
Dear H, E, J, and M—

I'm not into numerology, but it strikes me that this date—11/9 feels as apocalyptic as did '9/11.' Feeling *fearful* for us and this country over (at least) the next few years, I can't turn to religion or a deity for support and reassurance. Instead, some of my Buddhist readings assuage my *fear*, if not my grief, today. Most helpful is Pema Chodron's book, *When Things Fall Apart*. Some sustaining thoughts for me are these:

> "…..*disassociating from fear is what we do naturally. We habitually spin off and freak out when there's even the merest hint of fear. We feel it coming and we check out.*"

> "*So, the next time you encounter fear, consider yourself lucky. This is where courage comes in. Usually we think that brave people have no fear. The truth is that they are intimate with fear.*"

*"The trick is to keep exploring and not bail out, even when we find out that something is not what we thought. That's what we're going to discover again and again. Nothing is what we thought. Things falling apart is a kind of testing and also a kind of healing... the truth is that things don't really get solved. They come together and they fall apart. Then they come together again and fall apart again. The healing comes from letting there be room (in our minds) for all of this to happen: room for grief, for relief, for misery, for joy. When there's a big disappointment, **we don't know if that's the end of the story**. It may be just the beginning of a great adventure."*

"Life is like that. We don't know anything. We call something bad: we call it good. But really we just don't know."

"Thinking that we can find some lasting pleasure and avoid pain is what in Buddhism (is called) the hopeless cycle that goes round and round endlessly, causing (all of our) suffering. From this point of view, the only time we ever know what's really going on is when the rug's been pulled out and we can't find anywhere to land. We use these situations to either wake us up (to relax, get mindful) or put ourselves to sleep."

"To stay with that shakiness – to stay with a broken heart, with a rumbling stomach, with the feeling of hopelessness and wanting to get revenge – that is the path... Sticking with that uncertainty, getting the knack of relaxing in the midst of chaos, learning not to panic –this is the path of the warrior."

And finally this from J. Kornfeld's *A Path with Heart*:

"A spiritual warrior takes everything as a challenge — an ordinary (person) takes everything as a blessing or a curse."

Maybe these thoughts help.

Love, Dad

www.ingramcontent.com/pod-product-compliance
Lightning Source LLC
Chambersburg PA
CBHW032105090426
42743CB00007B/245